BEST OF
Florence

Damien Simonis

How to use this book

Colour-Coding & Maps

Each chapter has a colour code along the banner at the top of the page, which is also used for text and symbols on maps (eg all venues reviewed in the Highlights chapter are orange on the maps). The fold-out maps inside the front and back covers are numbered from 1 to 7. All sights and venues in the text have map references; eg (4, D3) means Map 4, grid reference D3. See p96 for map symbols.

Prices

Multiple prices listed with reviews (eg €) 10/5) usually indicate adult/concession admission to a venue. Concession prices can include senior, student, member or coupon discounts. Meal cost and room rate categories are listed at the start of the Eating and Sleeping chapters, respectively.

Text Symbols

- ☎ telephone
- ✉ address
- 🖳 email/website address
- € admission
- 🕑 opening hours
- ⓘ information
- 🚌 bus
- Ⓟ parking available
- ♿ wheelchair access
- ✗ on-site/nearby eatery
- 👶 child-friendly venue
- Ⓥ good vegetarian selection

Best of Florence
2nd edition – May 2006
First published – May 2003

Published by Lonely Planet Publications Pty Ltd
ABN 36 005 607 983

Australia Head Office, Locked Bag 1, Footscray, Vic 3011
☎ 03 8379 8000, fax 03 8379 8111
🖳 talk2us@lonelyplanet.com.au
USA 150 Linden St, Oakland, CA 94607
☎ 510 893 8555, toll free 800 275 8555
fax 510 893 8572
🖳 info@lonelyplanet.com
UK 72–82 Rosebery Ave, Clerkenwell, London
EC1R 4RW
☎ 020 7841 9000, fax 020 7841 9001
🖳 go@lonelyplanet.co.uk

This title was commissioned in Lonely Planet's London office and produced by: **Commissioning Editor** Michala Green **Coordinating Editors** Sarah Hassall, Margedd Heliosz **Coordinating Cartographer** Jimi Ellis **Layout Designer** Kaitlin Beckett **Cartographers** Julie Sheridan, Sarah Sloane **Managing Cartographer** Mark Griffiths **Cover Designer** Daniel New **Project Managers** Glenn van der Knijff, Fabrice Rocher **Mapping Development** Paul Piaia **Desktop Publishing Support** Mark Germanchis **Thanks to** Stephanie Pearson, Jennifer Garrett, Tasmin McNaughtan, Fayette Fox, Imogen Hall, Wendy Wright, Nicola Williams

Photographs by Lonely Planet Images and Juliet Coombe except for the following: p5, p7, p9, p10, p15, p16, p18, p20, p21, p26, p27, p28, p29, p30, p35 (upper), p37, p39, p52, p53, p54, p57, p58, p59, p61, p64, p65, p76, p77, p79 Martin Hughes/Lonely Planet Images; p14 Hannah Levy; p17 John Elk III; p22 Oliver Strewe; p23 Glenn Beanland; p24 Russell Mountford; p25, p38 Damien Simonis; p36 Ryan Fox; p40 John Hay; p71 Martin Moos. **Cover photograph** The Modern artist Boboli Gardens (Giardino di Boboli) were created in the mid-16th century around the Pitti Palace (Palazzo Pitti) in Florence, Juliet Coombe/Lonely Planet Images. All images are copyright of the photographers unless otherwise indicated. Many of the images in this guide are available for licensing from Lonely Planet Images: www.lonelyplanetimages.com.

ISBN 1 74059 679 X

Printed through The Bookmaker International Ltd.
Printed in China

Contents

From the Publisher

AUTHOR
Damien Simonis

Ever since he put down his bags in an Oltrarno apartment for a stint back in 1999, Damien has shuttled back and forth to Florence regularly. Conscious (and even frustrated!) that it would take a lifetime to unlock the place's 1001 secrets, artistic and otherwise, despite its modest size, he keeps digging around for new marvels. For this edition he went a little upmarket and chose to live in Corso Italia – getting yet another perspective on life on the Arno. Thanks go to Monica Fontani and Matteo Benvenuti, Luisa De Salvo, Fabiana Boccuni, Michela d'Ippolito, Barbara dall'Acqua, Fabrizio Gesi, Alessandra Parini and Dr Luca Bardi, Martino Bruni, Alessandro Finardi and family, Lucia Montigiani and William fforde, Cristiana Vannini. Special thanks to Massimo Vanni for the all the intown lowdown. And above all to Janique LeBlanc, *merci!*

The 1st edition of this book was written by Martin Hughes.

PHOTOGRAPHER
Juliet Coombe

As a full-time freelance travel photo-journalist, Juliet has taken pictures that have appeared in more than 200 Lonely Planet guidebooks and over 400 magazines worldwide. She has recently won the prestigious Australian Travel Photographer of the Year 2005 for her image of the Venice Carnival and British Guild of Travel Writers award for Travel Photographer of the Year in 2004. Her images have also been published in the *New York Times*, *Geographical* magazine, *Marie Claire* and *House and Garden*. Juliet finds that, in Florence she can enjoy the finer things in life: everything is art, even the way they make their ice cream!

Introducing Florence

Imagine what life would be like without Florence. If the little city on the River Arno hadn't defeated its rivals to become the capital of Tuscany and – keen to brag about its successes – hadn't unleashed that artistic spurt known as the Renaissance. What kind of world would we have inherited if it hadn't been coloured by the likes of Giotto, Leonardo da Vinci, Michelangelo, Dante and Donatello (just to snap the tip off the iceberg)?

Florence, quite simply, is like no other place on earth. There may be other conveniently compact and beautifully preserved medieval cities with glorious architecture, terracotta-tiled roofs, elegant bridges and unforgettable sunsets, but nowhere else is there such a staggering concentration of the world's most beautiful artworks, by a roll-call of such impressive names. Toss in some of the world's greatest cooking and a case or two of its finest wines and you begin to see why Florentines appear so self-assured. Add a layer of impeccable fashion sense together with a gene pool that seems to create nothing but lookers and the smugness of the people seems unfairly well placed. As they say, if you've got it, flaunt it!

Ah yes, but *we* mere mortals can go to Florence; if the Florentines live in this veritable paradise, where can they go for respite and inspiration? Oh yeah…Tuscany…with its blissful vineyards, medieval hill-top villages, creamy-coloured villas, unforgettable vistas and every other magical image the very mention of its name evokes.

Imagine coming back as a Florentine…

Art abounds in museums – and many private galleries – throughout Florence

Neighbourhoods

Florence, nestled on the banks of the Arno and contained by the foothills of the Apennines, is remarkably compact and easily negotiable by foot. Most sights are in and around the **Centro Storico** (historic centre) – or medieval core – the bulk of which is shown on Map 4.

The Duomo is the de facto centre and you can see its dome from points all over the city. The main train station is in Santa Maria Novella, to the west, while the **San Marco** area and the Galleria dell'Accademia (home to Michelangelo's *David)* are a short walk north. South down Via dei Calza-iuoli is Piazza della Signoria, dominated by the medieval Palazzo Vecchio. If you headed east from here you'd quickly reach Santa Croce, but you'll probably walk through the Uffizi for a close-up of the breathtakingly romantic Ponte Vecchio. Over the bridge is the less developed and more pleasant **Oltrarno** ('beyond the Arno'), which quickly gives way to hills and ledges perfect for city views. The Oltrarno boasts several key sights, including the Cappella Brancacci but also has a more genuine, workaday Florentine feel about it. It also offers some wonderful, atmospheric places to eat and drink.

Inevitably you'll be drawn to spend most time north of the Arno. Where to start? The city core is jammed with art and architecture. The great basilicas form an artistic arc around the centre, from **Santa Croce** in the east (around which are plenty of restaurants and bars) via **San Lorenzo** to **Santa Maria Novella** near the train station. Art lovers will include the Museo Nazionale del Bargello and Museo dell'Opera del Duomo on their lists, while shoppers will make for chic Via de' Tornabuoni.

OFF THE BEATEN TRACK

Escape the camcorders and bum bags by taking what feels like a country stroll up the winding roads behind the eatery, Enoteca Fuoriporta in the San Niccolò area of Oltrarno. Another beautiful, country-style stroll would have you following Via di San Leonardo south from the Forte di Belvedere. For still more fresh air, try the Parco delle Cascine. Want to see some art but without the Hawaiian shirts and gee whiz! brigade? Try the Chiesa di San Miniato al Monte, Cenacolo di Santo Spirito, Cenacolo di Foligno, Chiesa e Convento di Santa Maria Maddalena de' Pazzi and Chiostro dello Scalzo.

Knock, knock, knocking on Piazza del Duomo

Itineraries

Forget that Florence is small and that most sights are within easy walking distance; even if you stay for a month, it won't be long enough to take everything in. If the Uffizi and the Galleria dell'Accademia are on your list, make a reservation. For €3 per museum, you can book in advance for 13 state museums *(musei statali)*, including the Uffizi, Palazzo Pitti, the Museo Nazionale del Bargello and Galleria dell'Accademia. Phone **Firenze Musei** (☎ 055 29 48 83; www.firenzemusei.it; ⏰ 8.30am-6.30pm Mon-Fri, 8.30am-12.30pm Sat).

So that's what they say about Museo di San Marco

> **FLORENCE LOWLIGHTS**
> - Rip-off merchants passing for restaurants in the historic quarter
> - Trying to squeeze past the crowds queuing in front of the Galleria dell'Accademia
> - Attractions that close early and just chuck you out
> - The summertime stink of some city streets

Day One

After checking out the Duomo (p10) and the Battistero (p11), spend the morning in relative peace in the Museo dell'Opera del Duomo (p13), followed by lunch at Gustavino (p52). Wander through the historic centre and over the Ponte Vecchio (p17) to the Cappella Brancacci (p18). Head up the hill to the Chiesa di San Miniato al Monte (p29) for sunset, then flop back down to superb wines and a meal at Enoteca Fuoriporta (p58).

Day Two

If you've made a reservation, join the crowds at the Uffizi (p8), after which you'll need a leisurely lunch at Frescobaldi (p52). For a change of pace, explore the labyrinth of Palazzo Vecchio (p20) before strolling over to Santa Croce and its basilica (p19). Hang around for food at Ristorante Cibrèo (p57) and drinks at Rex Caffè (p64).

Day Three

Start the day by making the acquaintance of Michelangelo's *David* at the Galleria dell'Accademia (p14) and follow up with a visit to the Museo di San Marco (p21). Head down to the Mercato Centrale area for lunch at Trattoria Mario (p54). Do some afternoon window-shopping around Via de' Tornabuoni before cocktails at Capoccaccia (p63). Cross the river for dinner at Ristorante Beccofino (p59).

Highlights

UFFIZI (4, E6)

When Cosimo I had the Galleria degli Uffizi built in the mid-16th century to house the new Tuscan administration (*uffizi* meaning 'offices'), he commandeered the light-filled top storey to display the bits and pieces of art his family had collected over the years. To enter what is now the world's oldest gallery is to be thrust head reeling, heart pumping and mouth watering into the core of the Renaissance and the greatest concentration of Florentine and Italian art on the planet.

INFORMATION
- ☎ 055 238 86 51 (information),
  055 29 48 83 (reservations)
- 💻 www.polomuseale.firenze.it/uffizi
- ✉ Piazzale degli Uffizi 6
- € €6.50 (plus €3 for advance booking)
- ⏱ 8.15am-6.50pm Tue-Sun
- ℹ no flash photography, audioguide
  for one/two people €4.65/6.20
- 🚌 B
- ♿ good
- 🍴 roof terrace café

But rewind; this is also the one sight on every visitor's checklist and gets so packed with oohing and aahing crowds that you can hardly point out your favourite work without stubbing your finger. Queuing for a ticket can take several hours, so make sure you book a slot in advance and are in the right head space to appreciate it. There's far too much to take in on one visit, so have a good idea of what you're looking for if you don't have time up your sleeve to return.

Start at Room 2, off the corridors lined with eminent busts and sculptures. The room is dominated by three *Madonna in Maestà* (Madonna in Majesty) altarpieces by the 13th century's best, Duccio di Buoninsegna, Cimabue and Giotto, which show the start of the transition from Gothic to the Renaissance. Room 7 contains works by pioneering early 15th-century

Even after 500 years the Medici's art collection in Uffizi is still revered

Florentine painters, including *Madonna col Bambino* (Madonna and Child), by Masaccio and his master, Masolino. Also here are Piero della Francesca's portraits of *Federico da Montefeltro* and *Battista Sforza,* two of the most recognisable faces of the Renaissance. Room 8 introduces Filippo Lippi, most compellingly with his *Madonna col Bambino e due Angeli* (Madonna with Child and Two Angels), in which he modelled the Madonna on the ravishingly beautiful nun he would later marry after giving up his vows.

In Room 10, Lippi's student Sandro Botticelli provides the Uffizi's most famous paintings, particularly the ethereal *La Nascita di Venere* (Birth of Venus) and *Allegoria della Primavera* (Allegory of Spring).

Leonardo da Vinci's famed *Annunciazione* (The Annunciation) and his unfinished *Adorazione dei Magi* (Adoration of the Magi) can be found in Room 15.

The *Tondo Doni,* depicting the Holy Family, is the only mannerist painting Michelangelo finished, and is in Room 25. In Room 26, Raphael – who flitted in and out of Florence in the early 16th century

The man behind the brush and chisel – Michelangelo

– seals the High Renaissance with his portrait of *Leone X* (Pope Leo X). Room 27 is dominated by the at times unsettling works of Florence's two main mannerist masters, Pontormo and Il Rosso Fiorentino.

Reflecting the relocation of artistic importance from Florence, the collection then moves on to the rest of Italy and Europe. Room 28 is full of Titians, including the voluptuous *Venere d'Urbino* (Venus of Urbino). Fans of the Flemish should check out Room 41 for works by Rubens and Van Dyck.

The floors below the present gallery have been cleared and are being renovated to double exhibition space. Already relocated down here are works by Caravaggio and other chiaroscuro painters. On the first floor, much of the archaeological collection (statues and so on) will be grouped with minor artworks organised by theme (such as the self-portraits now in the Corridoio Vasariano). A new ground floor restaurant will open on the Arno side of the building. The project will not be completed before 2007.

DUOMO (4, E3)

The majestic dome of the medieval Duomo (cathedral) is a symbol of Florence and easily visible from points around the city.

Although the first stones were laid by Arnolfo di Cambio in 1296, the building processes continued for another 150 years. Brunelleschi jumped at the opportunity to cap it with the world's largest dome, which was completed in 1436.

Arnolfo's original, only partially completed, front façade was torn down in the late 16th century by city fathers and only replaced in 1888 with Emilio de Fabris' neo-Gothic frontage.

The interior itself feels arrestingly austere (wealthy Florentines really only wanted to dazzle visitors their money – they themselves didn't need reminding). Interesting features include *Dante e I Suoi Mondi* (Dante and His Worlds), the most reproduced image of the author of the *Divina Commedia* (Divine Comedy).

The views beneath the dome are just as spectacular as those from outside, as it frames one of the world's largest frescoed surfaces, painted by Giorgio Vasari and Federico Zuccaro in the 16th century.

Between the left (northern) arm of the transept and the apse is the **Sagrestia delle Messe** (Mass Sacristy), with exquisite inlaid wood panelling. The bronze doors, by Luca della Robbia, were Lorenzo de' Medici's escape route when he fled an assassination attempt in 1478.

Donatello, Ghiberti and others created the magnificent stained glass that adorns the windows. You can get a closer look by climbing the steep steps inside the Dome from a door outside on the church's north flank. You can also visit the **crypt**.

INFORMATION

- ☎ 055 230 28 85
- ✉ Piazza del Duomo
- € cathedral free; dome €6; crypt €3
- ⏰ cathedral 10am-5pm Mon-Wed & Fri, 10am-3.30pm Thu, 10am-4.45pm Sat, 1-4.45pm Sun; dome 8.30am-7pm Mon-Fri, 8.30am-5.40pm Sat; crypt 10am-5pm Mon-Wed & Fri, 10am-3.30pm Thu, 10am-4.45pm Sat
- 🚌 1, 6, 7, 10, 11, 14, 17, 23 & A
- ♿ good (to cathedral only)
- ✗ Caffè Coquinarius (p52)

DON'T MISS

- Giovanni de' Medici's sword in the crypt
- The monument to the English mercenary John Hawkwood
- The view of the marble pavement as you climb into the dome

BATTISTERO (4, D3)

The 12th-century Battistero (baptistry) – possibly built on the site of a Roman temple – is best known for the gilded bronze doors that Michelangelo called the **Porta del Paradiso** (Gates of Paradise).

At the start of the 15th century a competition was held between leading artists to create a set of doors for the northern entrance with panels depicting scenes from the New Testament. The trial panels of Brunelleschi and a 23-year-old Lorenzo Ghiberti were so innovative that they are often regarded as the first products of the Renaissance. The impressed judging committee awarded the two artists a joint contract, but a hot-headed Brunelleschi packed off to Rome and left Ghiberti to toil on the doors for 21 years. The commissioning guild was so rapt with the results – which showed Ghiberti's burgeoning mastery of perspective – that they sent him back to produce another set. Twenty-seven years later, Ghiberti emerged with the 10 panels that so moved Michelangelo. Eight of the restored originals – the ones here are copies – are exhibited in the Museo dell'Opera del Duomo (p13).

INFORMATION

- ☎ 055 230 28 85
- 🖥 www.operaduomo.firenze.it
- ✉ Piazza di San Giovanni
- € €3
- 🕙 noon-7pm Mon-Sat, 8.30am-2pm Sun & holidays
- 🚌 1, 6, 7, 10, 11, 14, 17, 23 & A
- ♿ good
- ✕ Ristorante Self-Service Leonardo (p53)

DON'T MISS

- Baldassare Cossa's tomb by Donatello and Michelozzo
- The exterior's Tuscan Romanesque green-and-white marble
- The bust of a balding Ghiberti on the East Doors
- Andrea Pisano's South Doors (1336)

Inside glittering, gold-ground mosaics line the vault and illustrate the *Last Judgement*. In the centre of the elaborate tessellated marble floor stood the font where many famous Florentines, including Dante, were baptised. They could clearly see the Damned above them (it looks like quite a party).

The stunning *Last Judgement* is awash with 13th-century gold-ground mosaics

CAMPANILE (4, E3)

While it's almost dwarfed on this piazza by the Duomo, don't overlook the beautifully beefy Campanile (bell tower) designed by Giotto – yes, the artist – in 1334 while he was city architect. It soars 85m above the piazza, is clad in the same white, green and pink marble as the Duomo, and is one of the most beautiful bell towers in Italy (and that's saying something).

INFORMATION

- ☎ 055 230 28 85
- 🖳 www.operaduomo.firenze.it
- ✉ Piazza del Duomo
- € €6
- ☾ 8.30am-7.30pm Apr-Sep, 9am-4.30pm Oct-Mar
- 🚌 1, 6, 7, 10, 11, 14, 17, 23 & A
- ✗ Caffè Coquinarius (p52)

Giotto died three years into its construction, when the Campanile was only about 13m high. It was completed in 1359, with some adjustments, by Andrea Pisano and Francesco Talenti, who doubled the thickness of the walls once they realised the tower was in danger of toppling over. It seems Giotto, while one of the greatest artists of his age, was not too flash as an engineer.

DYNAMIC DAEDALUS

Near the base of the Campanile, look for the relief depicting Daedalus – the mythical Athenian architect, sculptor and inventor – soaring with the help of his homemade wings, a fitting symbol for the Renaissance.

Apart from its size and striking façade, the Campanile is best known for its decoration. There are 16 sculptures of prophets and patriarchs (by Donatello, among others) and bas-reliefs (possibly designed by Giotto), which provide a veritable encyclopaedia of medieval thinking, depicting everything from the arts to the planets.

Up 414 lung-busting steps you reach a terrace at the top of the Campanile with splendid views of Florence and, particularly, the Duomo's dome.

Giotto – as an architect – put the Campanile bell tower into perspective ....

MUSEO DELL'OPERA DEL DUOMO (4, F3)

The most gratifying museum in Florence – not least because it seems to be overlooked by the tourist herds – the Museo dell'Opera del Duomo, recently remodelled, light and airy, exhibits the sculptural treasures that once adorned the buildings of the Duomo complex.

Head straight for the courtyard and the display of Ghiberti's original panels from the Battistero (p11). The first room proper is filled with relics from Arnolfo di Cambio's original Duomo façade, along with ruined bits and bobs from Etruscan and Roman times, and a collection of saintly relics, including the index finger of John the Baptist.

On the landing of the stairs is one of our favourite Renaissance treasures (and without doubt the museum's best-known piece), the *Pietà* that Michelangelo had intended for his own tomb and which became his obsession late in life. Dissatisfied with the flawed marble and his own fallibility, he took a hammer to Christ in the first recorded instance of an artist vandalising his own work. He destroyed the arm and left leg. The figure of Nicodemus, futilely supporting the dead Christ, is Michelangelo's self-portrait, and the unfinished work is one of the most poignant ever crafted.

The other major highlights for art lovers and tourists alike are upstairs, where the *cantorie*, two contrasting marble choir stalls made in the 1430s by Luca della Robbia and Donatello, among the most exquisitve works of the age. Luca Della Robbia's panels depict angelic children dancing and frolicking, while Donatello's portray children racing and cavorting with frenzied abandon, jumping out from a mosaic background.

Other exhibits include the original reliefs from the Campanile as well as assorted models and plans.

INFORMATION
- ☎ 055 230 28 85
- ✉ Piazza del Duomo 9
- € €6
- ⏰ 9am-7.30pm Mon-Sat, 9am-1.40pm Sun
- ℹ no flash photography; audioguide €4
- 🚌 14 & 23
- ♿ good
- ✗ Caffellatte (p53)

DON'T MISS
- Brunelleschi's death mask
- Donatello's dramatic – and hideous – wooden Mary Magdalene
- The tools used by Brunelleschi in the construction of the Duomo

GALLERIA DELL'ACCADEMIA (7, A1)

Every visitor to Florence wants to clap eyes on Michelangelo's *David:* history's most famous sculpture, housed here in the world's first formal academy of art and architecture, set up by Cosimo I in 1562.

INFORMATION
- ☎ 055 238 86 09
- ✉ Via Ricasoli 60
- € €6.50
- ◷ 8.15am-6.50pm Tue-Sun
- ▣ C
- ♿ good
- ✖ Il Vegetariano (p54)

Galleria dell'Accademia's most famous resident – Michelangelo's *David*

Crowds crush inside and outside this gallery and it's difficult to appreciate Michelangelo's genius with people taking photographs and stewards yelling at them to stop.

Your heart will fill with joy when you first see *David,* sculpted by Michelangelo from 1501 to 1504 from a long, narrow piece of previously scorned marble. From the awkward block he carved the largest statue since Roman times, a unique and powerful 4.34m-high depiction of the biblical giant-slayer, intended as a symbol of the new Florentine Republic's liberty. It stood in Piazza della Signoria, where its arm was knocked off during a political insurrection – you can see the break – and was moved here in 1873.

To see *David* you raced past Michelangelo's four *Prigioni* (Slaves), unfinished sculptures of strapping figures struggling to free themselves Intending them for the tomb of Pope Julius II, Michelangelo abandoned them for a 'little' job on the Sistine Chapel.

The other major sculptural highlight in the Galleria dell'accademia is a plaster model of Giambologna's *Ratto delle Sabine* (Rape of the Sabine Women), for many said to be the best mannerist sculpture in existence. Other exhibition rooms contain countless sculptural reproductions, a mishmash of late-Gothic and Renaissance art and would you believe, an outstanding collection of old musical instruments.

DAVID TAKES A BATH
In 2003 a storm broke out over whether or not Michelangelo's *David* was in need of a good scrubbing down. After centuries exposed to the elements in Piazza della Signoria and an unfortunate acid-based clean in the 19th century, restorers fell out after 10 years of study over the best method to adopt. In the end David was gently washed down (the alternative was a careful brushing of the marble) and scrubbed up nicely for the public in 2004.

MUSEO NAZIONALE DEL BARGELLO (4, F5)

What the Uffizi is to painting, the Bargello is to Renaissance sculpture. Its outstanding anthology ranges from key works by masters such as Michelangelo, Donatello and Giambologna to a superb collection of decorative arts, glazed terracotta by the renowned della Robbia family, oriental rugs and ivory pieces from the 5th to the 17th century.

Built in the mid-13th century, it was the police (the Bargello) headquarters and city jail until 1859.

The first room is dedicated to Michelangelo and his followers, starting with his drunken *Bacchus,* playfully mocking the classic poses of ancient works, and moving on through the charming *Tondo Pitti,* an unfinished Apollo, and Michelangelo's only bust, *Brutus.* Benvenuto Cellini's large bust, *Cosimo I,* commands attention even in this exalted company, while Giambologna's nimble-footed *Mercurio Volante* (Mercury) arguably steals the show.

Upstairs in the magnificent hall, Donatello's very suave and effeminate bronze *David* looks like he might have charmed Goliath into submission. It's interesting to compare it to his earlier works, including a very different marble *David,* a gallant *San Giorgio* (St George) that once graced the façade of Chiesa di Orsanmichele, and the heraldic lion, *Marzocco.* Don't miss the sample panels Ghiberti and Brunelleschi produced for the Battistero doors competition – the first rumblings of the Renaissance.

INFORMATION

- ☎ 055 238 86 06
- ✉ Via del Proconsolo 4
- € €4
- ⊙ 8.15am-1.50pm Tue-Sat, also alternating Sun & Mon
- 🚌 14, 23 & A
- ♿ fair
- ✖ Vini e Vecchi Sapori (p53)

DON'T MISS

- The exquisite works of the della Robbia family
- The Islamic tapestries, Renaissance jewellery, ivory and armour
- Donatello's different bust of *Niccolò da Uzzano*
- The frescoes in the Cappella di Santa Maria Maddalena

There's more than one staircase to sculptural heaven at Museo Nazionale del Bargello

BASILICA DI SAN LORENZO (4, D2)

This bustling area was the original stomping ground of the ruling Medici, who lavished their wealth – well, a teeny weeny portion of it – on this their parish church, rebuilt by Brunelleschi from 1425 and one of the most splendid examples of Renaissance architecture you'll see.

INFORMATION

☎ 055 21 66 34
✉ Piazza San Lorenzo
€ €2.50
🕑 church 10am-5pm Mon-Sat; library closed at time of writing
🚌 1, 6, 7, 10, 11, 14, 17, 23 & A
🍴 Trattoria Mario (p54)

Inspired interior of Basilica di San Lorenzo

Behind the blank façade hides a little-known work by Michelangelo, the *Balcony of the Holy Relics*, the distinctive Medici family crest with six balls on a shield. ('Balls, balls, balls' was the Medici rallying cry.) Beneath the beautiful coffered ceiling towards the transept are two dark bronze pulpits, Donatello's last works upon which he toiled until his death. Try focusing in the dim light and you'll see moving scenes depicting the *Passions of Christ*.

Donatello decorated his friend Brunelleschi's impressive quadrangular Sagrestia Vecchia. The four corner roundels were modelled with wet plaster (a method soon made redundant by the glazed terracotta of Luca della Robbia). A 1989 restoration revealed the sculptor's fingerprints. He is buried close to his patron, Cosimo, founder of the Medici dynasty, whose humble tomb is marked by a slab in front of the altar.

An entrance left of the church leads to the tranquil cloisters and the vestibule to the Biblioteca Medicea Laurenziana via Michelangelo's *pietra serena* (grey 'tranquil stone') staircase. Architectural features, such as walled-in windows and columns that carry no weight, serve as mere decoration.

DON'T MISS
• Filippo Lippi's *Annunciazione* (Annunciation)
• Fiorentino's *Sposalizio della Vergine* (Marriage of the Virgin)
• Pietro Annigoni's *San Giuseppe Artigiano con Cristo* (St Joseph and Christ in the Workshop), a rare 20th-century highlight

PONTE VECCHIO (4, D6)

One of the most famous crossings in the world, the Ponte Vecchio (Old Bridge) was built in 1345 on the narrowest point of the River Arno. Although the Arno looks pretty placid, it can get mean, and washed away two previous stone incarnations in the floods of 1177 and 1333. The deluge of 1966 also threatened the bridge but the flood precautions – some designed by Leonardo da Vinci – held tight. More remarkably, it was the only bridge not blown to smithereens in WWII by the retreating Germans, who apparently decided that bombing the icon would have been a bridge too far, so they mined both sides instead.

The original workshops on the bridge were stinky tanneries and butchers, but these were cleared soon after the construction of the Corridoio Vasariano (Vasari Corridor). Grand Duke Ferdinando I de' Medici preferred glitter to gore and replaced them with the more decorous jewellers that continue to ply their trade here today. The bust in the centre of the bridge is of Benvenuto Cellini (1500–71), the most famous Florentine blacksmith, and was placed here in 1900.

> **PONTE VECCHIO VISTAS**
> You'll get an eyeful from the bridge but the place to pitch yourself and your camera for views of the Ponte Vecchio are the Ponte Santa Trinita just before sunset, or up close from the Hotel Lungarno's terrace, just off Borgo San Jacopo in Oltrarno. Classic morning views are from Piazzale Michelangelo and, much closer up, from inside the Uffizi.

Packed by day with camera-clicking tourists, hawkers and the occasional determined local in transit, the Ponte Vecchio is nevertheless one of the most cherished Florentine icons and a memorable place to linger.

Memories are made of this – the River Arno and Ponte Vecchio at sunset

CAPPELLA BRANCACCI (3, B7)

The ideal place to begin your tour of Renaissance art, this gorgeous chapel near Piazza Santo Spirito contains an extraordinary cycle of vivid frescoes that many believe kick-started the whole Renaissance painting she-bang.

> ### INFORMATION
> ☎ 055 276 82 24
> ✉ Via Santa Monaca
> € €4 (combined ticket with Palazzo Vecchio €8)
> 🕑 10am-5pm Wed-Mon, 1-5pm Sun & holidays
> ⓘ enter along the right side of Basilica di Santa Maria del Carmine; no flash
> 🚃 D
> 🍴 Trattoria Napoleone (p60)

The St Peter frescoes were a collaborative effort by Masolino and his precocious pupil Masaccio, who is credited with making the definitive break from the Gothic style by fusing humanism and perspective, and plunging into the new worlds of expression. Masaccio worked on the frescoes alone for a year, before following his master to Rome. He died soon after, aged just 27, unaware that he had changed the course of art forever. Filippino Lippi finished the cycle 60 years later, after the exiled Brancacci returned to Florence.

> ### SPARED THE BLAZE
> That the Cappella Brancacci survives at all is something of a miracle. Every other part of Basilica di Santa Maria del Carmine was destroyed by fire in 1771, after which this bombastic Baroque version was thrown up.

You could spend hours contemplating the frescoes, but start by comparing Masolino's demure *Tentazione di Adamo e Eva* (Temptation of Adam and Eve), on the right, with Masaccio's harrowing *Cacciata dei Progenitori* (Expulsion of Adam and Eve), opposite. Masaccio, obviously on a roll, took just four days to create one of the most powerful and moving images in the history of art. Fig leaves protecting original man and woman's modesty – painted on at the insistence of church authorities – were removed when the frescoes were restored in the 1980s.

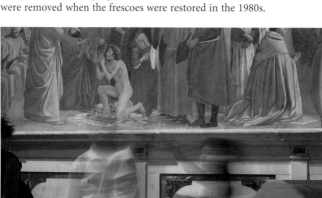

Time for reflection on the famed frescoes of the Cappella Brancacci

BASILICA DI SANTA CROCE (7, B5)

One of the city's most handsome churches, Santa Croce is as well known for its funerary monuments to Florence's highest achievers, including Michelangelo and Galileo, as for its artistic gems. It's where the protagonists of EM Forster's *A Room with a View* stumbled upon one another and where the French writer Stendhal first started feeling wobbly.

Built by the powerful Franciscan order, it was designed by the prolific Arnolfo di Cambio and completed in the mid-15th century. The attractive, and comparatively restrained, façade is a 19th-century neo-Gothic add-on by Nicola Matas, who pretended to have found original designs in the church archive to get the gig.

Past the scowling Dante at the entrance and the unexceptional monument to Michelangelo on the right – you'll see Donatello's gilded although cast in grey *pietra serena, Annunciazione* (Annunciation). Around the dogleg is the Baroncelli family's private chapel with delightful frescoes – the first depicting a night scene – by Taddeo Gaddi. The Bardi and Peruzzi chapels are decorated with fragmented frescoes by Giotto who, unfortunately painted them on dry instead of wet plaster, thus contributing to their poor condition.

INFORMATION
- ☎ 055 246 61 05
- ✉ Piazza Santa Croce 16
- € €4/2 (includes museum; p26)
- 🕑 9.30am-5.30pm Mon-Sat, 1-5.30pm Sun Apr-Oct;9.30am-12.30pm & 3-5.30pm Mon-Sat, 3-5.30pm Sun Nov-Mar
- ℹ no flash photography; audioguide €3
- 🚌 C
- 🍴 Osteria de' Benci (p57)

Daunting Dante, Basilica di Santa Croce

On the altar's far side is Donatello's *Crucifix*, in which his friend Brunelleschi reckoned he made Christ like a peasant. In an attempt to restore the Saviour's dignity Brunelleschi crafted his own, which now hangs in the Basilica di Santa Maria Novella.

The church's undisputed highlight is the serene and monumental **Cappella de' Pazzi** (Pazzi Chapel), a masterpiece of Renaissance architecture designed by Brunelleschi and decorated with characteristic glazed terracotta by Luca della Robbia.

DON'T MISS
- The tomb of Machiavelli
- Lingering a while in Brunelleschi's peaceful cloister
- Giotto's frescoes in the Bardi and Peruzzi chapels
- The statue of local girl Florence Nightingale

PALAZZO VECCHIO (4, E6)

The 95m-high bell tower of the fortress-like and rhomboid-shaped Palazzo Vecchio (Old Palace) soars above Piazza della Signoria and is yet another famous emblem of Florence.

INFORMATION

- ☎ 055 276 82 24
- ✉ Piazza della Signoria
- € €6 (combined ticket with Cappella Brancacci €8)
- ☾ 9am-7pm Fri-Wed, 9am-2pm Thu
- ⓘ audioguide €4.50; Museo dei Ragazzi (Children's Museum; p36)
- 🚌 B
- ♿ good
- ✗ Frescobaldi (p52)

There's much more to Palazzo Vecchio

The palace was built by Arnolfo di Cambio early in the 14th century and has been the seat of civic authority ever since. The interior got its mannerist makeover from Medici favourite Giorgio Vasari in 1540 when Cosimo I temporarily moved in. Vasari used to boast about how quickly he could churn out art and a bitchy Michelangelo once quipped that his haste showed in the results. Vasari is largely responsible for the ostentatious decoration in the **Salone dei Cinquecento** (Hall of the Five Hundred) which, although built to house the Republican government of Savonarola (p75), was turned into a grandiose expression of Medici power in the 1560s.

Upstairs is a series of rooms dedicated to pagan deities and a walkway across the top of the hall into the apartments of Cosimo I's wife, Eleanora, where you can see her chapel decorated by Bronzino.

The **Sala dei Gigli** houses the Palazzo's greatest treasure, Donatello's bronze masterpiece *Giuditta e Oloferne* (Judith and Holofernes; 1457), depicting the expressionless biblical heroine about to decapitate a drunken Holofernes, and meant to symbolise Humility's victory over Pride. When the Medici were temporarily banished in 1495, Savonarola's government placed it under the Loggia della Signoria (where a copy now stands) with a new base and inscription warning tyrants what they could expect.

MICHELANGELO WOZ 'ERE

Carved into the front wall of the Palazzo Vecchio, close to the Uffizi, is a curious little figure. Locals claim it's Michelangelo's work, done with his back to the wall and his hands behind his back to win a bet. Others say it's a quick self-portrait. Soon after he did it big fines were introduced to dissuade people from indulging in such graffiti habits on the walls of public buildings.

MUSEO DI SAN MARCO (3, E4)

This enthralling museum occupies the deconsecrated 13th-century convent of San Marco and is dedicated to the monk Guido di Pietro, whose religious art was so inspired he came to be known as Fra Angelico (1400–55).

In the 15th century Cosimo invited the Dominicans to town and got architect, Michelozzo, to redesign the beautiful buildings and cloister (built around an ancient cedar tree). Fra Angelico lived here from 1436 to 1447 when he, shall we say, 'decorated' the place.

First right on entering the soothing cloister – with corner frescoes by Angelico – is the **Sala dell'Ospizio** (Pilgrims' Hospice) now home to many of his works. Linger over his early *Ultima Cena* (Last Supper) altarpiece and the delightful *Trentacinque Scene dalla Vita del Cristo* (Thirty-five Scenes from the Life of Christ), which started out as cupboard doors.

A charming upstairs loggia displays the *Annunciazione* (Annunciation). The most moving works are in the 44 tiny white vaulted cells, each adorned with a fresco by Angelico and his assistants to inspire the lonely monks in prayer.

Past Michelozzo's beautifully colonnaded library are two cells reserved for Cosimo in times of spiritual need. The other end of the corridor contains the offices of Savonarola, that nasty piece of work who was made prior here in 1491.

INFORMATION

- ☎ 055 238 86 08
- ✉ Piazza San Marco 1
- € €4
- ⏰ 8.15am-1.50pm Tue-Fri, 8.15am-6.50pm Sat, 8.15am-7pm alternate Sun, 8.15am-1.50pm alternate Mon
- 🚌 6, 7, 10, 20, 25, 31, 32, 33 & C
- ♿ fair
- 🍴 Il Vegetariano (p54)

DON'T MISS

- *Madonna delle Ombre* (Madonna of the Shadows) to the right of cell No 25
- *Crocifissione,* which Fra Angelico is said to have painted through tears
- Fra Bartolommeo's Portrait of *Savonarola*

Chubby cherubs pay homage to Fra Angelico at Museo di San Marco

PALAZZO PITTI (4, B9)

Dominating the Oltrarno is the colossal Palazzo Pitti which houses five museums, including the Galleria Palatina and its vast collection of 16th- to 18th-century art amassed by the various people who called this place home.

Going for gold in the Palazzo Pitti

The original, narrower *palazzo* was designed by Brunelleschi in 1457 for the politically ambitious Luca Pitti, who was keen to thumb his nose at the ruling Medici – ironically, it was the wife of Cosimo I de' Medici who bought the place when the Pitti clan went bust a century later. It served as home base for Florence's rulers up until the Austrian House of Lorraine shipped out in 1868, and the building was extended several times – while respecting the original design – to accommodate their ever-increasing art collections. Ammanati designed the magnificent, oversized courtyard in the mid-16th century, while the unusual sloping forecourt is a 1996 addition and a popular spot to picnic, hang out or just lean forward.

The **Galleria Palatina** consists of 28 lavish but often dimly lit rooms crammed with a jumble of paintings in original gilt frames (see the 'Don't Miss' boxed text, for a selection of works to look out for). They are stacked up to five-high on damask walls and it can all get a bit overwhelming.

Your ticket also gets you into the **Appartamenti Reali** (Royal Apartments), used to meet and greet illustrious guests who probably – we suspect – at the very least suffered from what can only be described as the poor taste on show. A minimalist's worst nightmare.

DON'T MISS

- Filippo Lippi (Sala di Prometeo)
- Caravaggio (Sala dell'Educazione di Giove)
- Titian and Velázquez (Sala dell'Illiade)
- Raphael (Sala di Saturno and Sala di Giove)
- Rubens (Sala di Marte)

Other major galleries well worth visiting include the Galleria d'Arte Moderna (p25), Museo degli Argenti (p26), Galleria del Costume (p25) and Museo delle Porcellane (p26).

BASILICA DI SANTA MARIA NOVELLA (4, B2)

This Gothic church, completed by the Dominicans in the 14th century, contains a handful of important works, including a seminal fresco by the young Masaccio that incorporated the emerging values of painting, sculpture and architecture and is a defining moment in the early Renaissance.

The beautiful façade combines Romanesque style on the lower level with Renaissance above. It was completed in stages in both the 14th and 15th centuries. The Gothic interior was designed by monks from the Dominican order (a group of keen participants in the Inquisition and rather fond of a little self-flagellation) and is suitably sombre.

Opposite the entrance is Masaccio's recently restored *Trinità*, the first instance where Brunelleschi's mathematical rules of perspective were applied to a painting. Beneath the cross, you can still see where Masaccio hammered a nail to establish the 'vanishing point'. The fresco was only rediscovered in 1861.

Suspended dramatically above the nave behind you is an otherworldly *Crocifissione* by Giotto.

Domenico Ghirlandaio painted the delightful frescoes round the back of the main altar around 1485. The bystanders in the images represent a veritable who's who of 15th-century Florentine life.

Immediately to the right of the choir, the **Cappella di Filippo Strozzi**

INFORMATION

- ☎ 055 21 59 18
- ✉ Piazza di Santa Maria Novella
- € €2.50/1.50
- ⏰ 9am-5pm Mon-Thu & Sat, 1-5pm Fri, Sun & holidays
- ℹ museum & cloisters are separate from the Basilica
- 🚌 1, 7, 10, 11, 14, 17, 22, 23, 36, 37 & A
- ♿ fair
- 🍴 Trattoria dei 13 Gobbi (p55)

Go Gothic at Basilica di Santa Maria Novella

(1502) features some of Filippino Lippi's finest work, while the **Cappella Gondi**, to the left, contains Brunelleschi's *Crocifissione* sans genitalia or loincloth. His only surviving wooden sculpture was created in response to the despised naturalism of Donatello's version in Santa Croce.

DON'T MISS

- Museo di Santa Maria Novella and cloisters (p27)
- The Chiostro Verde (Green Cloister; p27), so-called due to the fading, green-based frescoes, especially those of *Il Diluvio Universale* (the Great Flood) by Paolo Uccello
- The Cappellone degli Spagnoli (Spanish Chapel; p27)

Sights & Activities

MUSEUMS & GALLERIES

Casa Buonarroti (7, B4)
Housed in a house that Michelangelo bought but never lived in, this over-priced museum (more like a memorial) was established by his descendants and features a few pieces by Michelangelo – including the marble relief *Madonna della Scala* (Madonna of the Steps; 1492), his earliest known work – along with drawings exhibited in rotation, other artists portraits of him, a few Etruscan urns and an overbearing security guard.
☎ 055 24 17 52 ⊠ Via Ghibellina 70 € €6.50
☼ 9.30am-2pm Wed-Mon
🚌 14 ♿ fair

Casa di Dante (4, E4)
This is not the house where Dante was born – it was built in the 20th century – but it is (or is near) the location where he lived. The recently renovated museum dedicated to Dante's work, life and times, contains pictures and models of 12th and 13th century Florence, completed by accounts of the interminable squabbles between Guelphs and Ghibellines and Dante's exile from the city.
☎ 055 21 94 16 ⊠ Via Santa Margherita 1 € €4/2
☼ 10am-5pm Tue-Sat, 10am-1pm Sun 🚌 A

Cenacolo di Foligno (3, C4)
Long forgotten until stumbled upon in the 19th century, this Last Supper scene is thought to have been done by students of the Umbrian Renaissance artist Il Perugino (1445–1523) to his design. The organisation of the scene is classic, with Judas (sans halo) sitting on the wrong side of the table, grasping the sack of coins. Ring the doorbell for entry.
☎ 055 28 69 82 ⊠ Via Faenza 42 € donation
☼ 9am-noon Mon, Tue & Sat 🚌 4, 12, 25, 31, 32 & 33

Cenacolo di Sant'Apollonia (3, D4)
If you're in the neighbourhood, duck into this former convent for a squiz at Andrea del Castagno's 15th-century fresco titled *Ultima Cena* (The Last Supper), found beneath coats of whitewash in the 19th century. He was one of the first artists to dabble with perspective.
☎ 055 238 86 07 ⊠ Via XXVII Aprile 1 € free
☼ 8.15am-1.50pm Tue-Sun & alternate Mon & Sun 🚌 7, 10, 20, 25, 31, 32 & 33 ♿ good

Loggia della Signoria (opposite): sculptures abound

Cenacolo di Santo Spirito (4, A7)
Home to the Fondazione Romano, a collection of 11th-century Romanesque sculpture, this former refectory provides a change of pace from the Renaissance and has grand frescoes by Andrea Orcagna depicting the Last Supper and the Crucifixion.
☎ 055 28 70 43 ⊠ Piazza di Santo Spirito 29 € €2.20
☼ 9am-2pm Tue-Sun

OPENING TIMES & TICKET TIPS

Opening times vary throughout the year, sometimes changing without warning from season to season. To be sure, get the updated list from the Azienda di Promozione Turistica (APT; p88) when you arrive. Many major museums close on Sunday afternoon and Monday, which is not very handy for a long weekend.

Ticket windows at most places shut 30 minutes before closing time. Also be aware that some places, such as Capella Brancacci, turn off the lights and shuffle you out early, while others start ringing their bells way in advance and make you feel rushed. Allow yourself plenty of time.

At busy times of the year you'd be bonkers to join the queues for the Uffizi or the Galleria dell'Accademia, which are long enough to ruin your holiday. For these, and any of the state museums, you can book ahead (see p7).

During Cultural Week, usually in April, all of Italy's state museums are free.

Apr-Nov, 10.30am-1.30pm Tue-Sun Dec-Mar 🚌 D

Chiostro dello Scalzo (3, E3)

You'd never guess what's inside this modest cloister (*chiostro*) of a church long gone. Pop along and treat yourself to the sounds of silence (few tourists make it here) and admire the sepia frescoes on the life and death of John the Baptist carried out in stop-start fashion by Andrea del Sarto throughout the course of his career.
✉ Via Cavour 69 € free
🕑 8.15am-1.50pm Mon, Thu & Sat 🚌 6, 7, 10, 20, 25, 31, 32, 33 & C

Galleria d'Arte Moderna (4, B9)

In Florentine art, 'modern' means from the end of the 18th century to the beginning of the 20th. The most interesting part – not necessarily the best – of this collection is the work of the Tuscan impressionists or late-19th-century Macchiaioli ('spot-makers').
☎ 055 238 86 16 ✉ Palazzo Pitti € €5 (combined ticket with Galleria del Costume) 🕑 8.15am-1.50pm Tue-Sat & alternating Sun & Mon 🚌 D

Galleria del Costume (4, A9)

This gallery on the ground floor of the Palazzo Pitti displays thousands of dresses that reflect the changing styles of court and high fashion from the late 1700s to the 1960s.
☎ 055 238 87 13 ✉ Palazzo Pitti € €5 (combined ticket with Galleria d'Arte Moderna) 🕑 8.15am-1.50pm Tue-Sat & alternating Sun & Mon 🚌 D 🕭 fair

Loggia del Bigallo (4, D3)

This minuscule museum attached to the Loggia del Bigallo (p34) has a few notable artworks, including the 14th-century *Madonna della Misericordia* fresco (in the Sala dei Capitani), which features the earliest known depiction of the city and the Duomo with its (at the time) incomplete façade.
☎ 055 230 28 85 ✉ Piazza San Giovanni 6 € €2
🕑 10am-6pm Wed-Mon
🚌 1, 6, 7, 10, 11, 14, 17, 23 & A

Loggia della Signoria (4, E6)

Built by Orcagna in the late 14th century as a platform for public ceremonies, this elegant arcade now serves as an open-air sculpture gallery, with highlights such as Cellini's magnificent bronze *Perseo* (Perseus) and (a copy of) Giambologna's Mannerist masterpiece *Ratto delle Sabine* (Rape of the Sabine Women). Also known as the Loggia dei Lanzi, the arcade was named after Cosimo I's Swiss mercenaries, the Lances, who were once stationed here.
✉ Piazza della Signoria
€ free 🕑 24hr 🚌 B

Macchine di Leonardo (4, E1)

Pop by here for a squiz at some grand-scale models of some of Leonardo da Vinci's more far-fetched ideas, silly things like flying machines, a bicycle, a

Loggia della Signoria and Palazzo Vecchio (p20)

Capture the serenity at Museo di Santa Maria Novella's (opposite) Chiostro Verde

glider, a tank and other objects that were, actually, centuries ahead of their time.

☎ 055 29 52 64 🖳 www .macchinedileonardo.com ✉ Via Cavour 21 € €5/4 🕙 9.30am-7pm 🚌 1, 6, 7, 10, 11, 14, 17, 23 & A

Museo Archeologico
(7, B2)

If you're at all interested in antiquity, you'll love this fabulous museum which was started by Cosimo I in the 15th century and exhibits include the outstanding collections of Etruscan, Greek, Roman and ancient Egyptian artefacts ranging from everyday items to classic ceremonial sculpture.

☎ 055 2 35 75 ✉ Via della Colonna 38 € €4 🕙 2-7pm Mon, 8.30am-7pm Tue & Thu, 8.30am-2pm Wed & Fri-Sun 🚌 6, 31, 32 & C ♿ excellent

Museo degli Argenti
(4, B8)

More than the silver in the name, this museum in Palazzo Pitti exhibits the massive private wealth of the Medici dynasty – at least, what wasn't sold off by the Lorraines

when they took over – and ranges from intricate jewellery to a chalice made from ostrich eggs. The centrepiece is a spectacular collection of antique *pietra dura* (semi precious stone) vases.

☎ 055 238 87 09 ✉ Palazzo Pitti € €4 with Giardino di Boboli & Museo delle Porcellane 🕙 8.15am-5.30pm Mar, 8.15am-6.30pm Apr-May & Sep-Oct, 8.15am-7.30pm Jun-Aug, 8.15am-4.30pm Nov-Feb; closed 1st and last Mon of each month 🚌 D

Museo dell'Antropologia e Etnologia
(4, F4)

Italy's first anthropology and ethnology museum is housed in the Palazzo Nonfinito (Unfinished Palace), which was started by Buontalenti in 1593 in the Mannerist style. It was established in 1869 and exhibits unusual goodies such as Ecuadorian shrunken heads and obscure musical instruments collected by roaming Italians.

☎ 055 239 64 49 ✉ Via del Proconsolo 12 € €4/2 🕙 9am-1pm Mon- & Tue & Thu & Fri, 9am-5pm Sat 🚌 14, 23 & A

Museo dell'Opera di Santa Croce
(7, B5)

To be included in your visit to the church, this austere museum contains several masterpieces salvaged – some only just – from the 1966 flood, including a restored crucifix by Cimabue and Donatello's gilded bronze statue of *San Ludovico di Tolosa* (St Ludovich of Toulouse), originally placed in a tabernacle on the façade of Orsanmichele.

☎ 055 246 61 05 ✉ Piazza di Santa Croce 16 € €4/2 (combined ticket with Basilica di Santa Croce) 🕙 9.30am-5.30pm Mon-Sat, 1-5.30pm Sun & holidays 🚌 C

Museo delle Porcellane
(3, C9)

Housed in the airy casino at the top of the Giardino di Boboli (p31), this museum contains a varied collection of fine porcelain, including fine pieces from Sèvres, Meissen and Vincennes, collected down the ages by illustrious tenants of Palazzo Pitti.

☎ 055 265 18 16 ✉ Giardino di Boboli € €4 (combined ticket with Giardino di Boboli) 🕙 8.15am-5.30pm

Mar, 8.15am-6.30pm
Apr-May & Sep-Oct, 8.15am-
7.30pm Jun-Aug, 8.15am-
4.30pm Nov-Feb; closed 1st
and last Mon of each month
🚌 D

Museo di Santa Maria Novella (4, B2)

Just to the left of the church
is the Chiostro Verde (Green
Cloister), one of the most
beautiful and tranquil spaces
in Florence, and so named
because Paolo Uccello used
a green earth pigment in his
frescoes, lending the place an
air of otherworldliness. There
are more wonderful frescoes,
by Andrea di Buonaiuto, in
the divinely serene Cappellone degli Spagnoli (Spanish
Chapel), which served as the
HQ for the Inquisition when it
came to town. The museum
itself has bits and bobs
removed from the church.
☎ 055 28 21 87 ✉ Piazza
di Santa Maria Novella
€ €2.70/2 🕙 9am-5pm
Mon-Thu & Sat, 9am-2pm
Sun & holidays 🚌 1, 7, 10,
11, 14, 17, 22, 23, 36, 37 & A
♿ good

Museo di Storia della Scienza (4, E7)

Perfect tonic for the art-
jaded tourist, this museum
is dedicated to Tuscany's
men of science, particularly
Galileo Galilei, whose telescope, lens and *finger* are on
display. In his memory, Florence founded an Academy
of Experimentation and you
can see early thermometers
and barometers invented by
the group, as well as gadgets
and innovations, including a
mechanical calculator.
☎ 055 26 53 11 ✉ Piazza
de' Giudici 1 € €6.50

🕙 9.30am-5pm Mon &
Wed-Fri, 9.30am-1pm Tue
& Sat Jun-Sep; 9.30am-5pm
Mon & Wed-Sat, 9.30am-
1pm Tue, 10am-1pm 2nd
Sun of every month Oct-May
🚌 23 & B ♿ excellent

Museo Horne (7, A5)

This pleasantly low-key
museum houses a collection
of 14th- and 15th-century
Italian paintings, sculptures,
ceramics, coins and other
odds and ends left to the
nation by British art his-
torian and Florentinophile
Herbert Percy Horne. Among
the relatively minor art,
you'll find the occasional
biggie such as Giotto's
Santo Stefano (St Stephen),
though the museum is
perhaps most interesting
for its exquisite array of
period furniture.

☎ 055 24 46 61 ✉ Via de'
Benci 6 € €5 🕙 9am-1pm
Mon-Sat 🚌 13, 23, B & C

Museo Marino Marini (4, B4)

If you have to ask 'who?' this
museum might not be for you.
Set in an ancient church, it has
almost 200 works by one of
Italy's best modern sculptors,
Marino Marini, whose world,
it seems, revolved around
man and horse.
☎ 055 21 94 32 ✉ Piazza
San Pancrazio 1 € €4
🕙 10am-5pm Mon-Fri,
Jun-Sep, 10am-5pm Mon-Sat
Oct-May 🚌 A ♿ good

Museo Salvatore Ferragamo (4, B5)

Housed on the 2nd floor of a
fortified Renaissance *palazzo*
that takes up an entire block,
this small museum displays

Museo di Santa Maria Novella: once home to the Inquisition

Spedale degli Innocenti's 'advertisement' for help for orphans

some 80 years of fashionable footwear produced by the Ferragamo empire, including many shoes that dressed the feet of film stars and princesses. You can pop in on spec but book to be sure. ☎ 055 336 04 56 🖥 www .salvatoreferragamo.it ✉ Via de' Tornabuoni 2 € free 🕑 9am-1pm & 2-6pm Mon-Fri 🚌 6, 11, 36, 37 & A

Museo Stibbert (1, E2)
Florence's most bizarre museum, is in a crumbling 14th-century Victorian-decorated *palazzo*, and contains the legacy of Federico Stibbert (1838–1906), fan of military paraphernalia and hoarder extraordinaire. Expect everything from a Botticelli painting and magnificent 16th- to 19th-century armour to quaint, curious and useless junk. There's a nice shady garden to rest and regain your composure. ☎ 055 47 55 20 ✉ Via Stibbert 26 € €5, gardens free

🕑 10am-2pm Mon-Wed, 10am-6pm Fri-Sun, gardens 10am-dusk 🚌 4

Museo Storico-Topograficao 'Firenze com'era' (7, A3)
The 'Florence as it was' museum charts the city's development – particularly from the Renaissance to today – with paintings, models, topographical drawings and prints. The most intriguing part are the pictures and models of the old city centre destroyed in the 19th century to make way for Piazza della Repubblica. ☎ 055 261 65 45 ✉ Via dell'Oriuolo 24 € €2.70 🕑 9am-2pm Fri-Wed 🚌 14 & 23

Museo Zoologico La Specola (4, A9)
The Medici founded this rather fusty museum in the 1770s; it has a vast collection of preserved and pickled animals, and a ghastly section strewn with

wax models of assorted and diseased bits of the human anatomy. ☎ 055 228 82 51 🖥 www .unifi.it/msn ✉ Via Romana 17 € €4 🕑 9am-1pm Thu & Fri & Sun-Tue, 9am-5pm Sat 🚌 11, 36, 37 & D

Opificio delle Pietre Dure (7, A1)
One of the most beautiful and overlooked of Florence's museums, this is attached to a workshop established by Ferdinando I in 1558 to create decorative pieces in *pietra dura* for the Cappelle Medicee. Now situated in the old convent of San Niccolò, it displays 19th-century workbenches and exquisite 'paintings in stones'. ☎ 055 26 51 11 ✉ Via degli Alfani 78 € €2 🕑 8.15am-2pm Mon-Wed & Fri-Sat, 8.15am-7pm Thu 🚌 C

Spedale degli Innocenti (7, A2)
Europe's first orphanage, opened in 1444, was Brunelleschi's first complete work as an architect. Andrea della Robbia decorated the elegant arcaded loggia with terracotta medallions of babies in swaddling clothes in the 1490s as an appeal for charity. Inside is Ghirlandaio's striking *Adorazione dei Magi* (Adoration of the Magi), along with an early and over-restored *Madonna col Bambino e un Angelo* (Madonna with Child and an Angel) by Botticelli. ☎ 055 249 17 08 ✉ Piazza Santissima Annunziata 12 € €4 🕑 8.30am-2pm Thu-Tue 🚌 6, 31, 32 & C

CHURCHES & CHAPELS

Badia Fiorentina (4, F5)
This 10th-century abbey has had a few too many renovations over the years but is still worth visiting to see Filippino Lippi's *Apparizione della Madonna a San Bernardo* (Appearance of the Virgin to St Bernard), to the left as you enter, through the small Renaissance cloister. The Romanesque bell tower got a mention from Dante.
✉ Via del Proconsolo ☾ 3-6pm Mon 🚌 14, 23 & A

Basilica di Santo Spirito (4, A7)
A barmy Baroque high altar, added in the 17th century, tends to distract from Brunelleschi's clean and harmonious design, although it's still easy to appreciate the colonnade of *pietra serena* columns and side chapels, which are filled with Renaissance art, including works by Domenico Ghirlandaio and Filippino Lippi.
☎ 055 21 00 30 ✉ Piazza di Santo Spirito ☾ 10am-

noon Mon-Fri & 4-5.30pm Thu-Tue 🚌 11, 36, 37 & D

Cappelle Medicee (4, D2)
The triumphalist mausoleum of the Medici was designed by Michelangelo in the 16th century but is still incomplete. Through the sober crypt is the **Cappella dei Principi** (Princes' Chapel), containing the six sarcophagi of Medici grand dukes and is lavish to the point of being loopy. The **Sagrestia Nuova** (New Sacristy) houses Mannerist sculptures by Michelangelo who, judging from the female figures, never saw a naked woman.
☎ 055 238 86 02 ✉ Piazza Madonna degli Aldobrandini € €6 ☾ 8.15am-5pm Tue-Sat & alternate Sun & Mon, 8.15am-1.50pm public holidays 🚌 1, 6, 7, 10, 11, 14, 17, 23 & A ♿ good

Chiesa di Ognissanti (3, B5)
This area was the old stomping ground of Amerigo Vespucci, and the young voyager is said to be pictured next to the Madonna in Ghirlandaio's fresco of the Madonna della Misericordia. Botticelli chips in with a fresco of St Augustine, while Ghirlandaio's masterful *Ultima Cena* (Last Supper)

adorns the wall of the *cenacolo* (refectory).
☎ 055 239 68 02 ✉ Borgo Ognissanti 42 ☾ church 7.30am-12.30pm & 3.30-7.30pm Mon-Sat, *cenacolo* 9am-noon Mon, Tue & Sat 🚌 A

Chiesa di Orsanmichele (4, D5)
This squat, 14th-century rectangle was originally a grain market but was deemed too good for the purpose and converted into a church. Most of the tabernacles on the exterior walls contain the original statues of the patron saints of Florence's various guilds, sculpted by the best 15th-century sculptors. Inside is a splendid 14th-century coloured-marble altar by Andrea Orcagna.
☎ 055 28 49 44 ✉ Via dell'Arte della Lana ☾ 9am-noon & 4-6pm, closed 1st & last Mon of month 🚌 A

Chiesa di San Miniato al Monte (3, F9)
The 11th-century treasure atop a hill in the Oltrarno is named after the city's first Christian martyr, who legend says flew up here decapitated head in hand. The Romanesque church boasts a multicoloured marble façade and, inside, a wealth of frescoes, mosaics and the

Chiesa di San Miniato al Monte

Renaissance **Cappella del Cardinale del Portogallo** (1466).
☎ 055 234 27 31 ⊠ Via delle Porte Sante € free, donations appreciated ☾ 8am-7.30pm May-Oct, 8am-noon & 3-6pm Nov-Apr 🚌 12 & 13

Chiesa di Santa Felicita
(4, C7)
This locals' church was built in 1736 to replace Florence's first – probably built in the 4th century – and incorporates part of Corridoio Vasariano (p33), which enabled the Medici to attend Mass without mingling with the mob. It's most famous today for the art of Mannerist painter Jacopo da Pontormo, particularly *Deposizione* (Deposition) and *Annunciazione* (Annunciation).
⊠ Via de' Guicciardini ☾ 9am-noon & 3-6pm Mon-Sat, 9am-1pm Sun 🚌 D ♿ fair

Chiesa di Santa Margherita (4, E4)
Dante fans will like to know that it was in this tiny 11th-century church, in the poet's old stomping ground, that he is said to have first espied his muse, Beatrice Portinari. And it is here that he ended up marrying Gemma Donati, to whom he had been promised.
⊠ Via Santa Margherita ☾ 10am-noon & 3-5pm 🚌 A

Chiesa di Santa Trinita
(4, B5)
This church was built in the 13th century and, although rebuilt in the Gothic style and later graced with an uninviting mannerist façade, you can get some idea of the Romanesque original from inside. Its most famous art is in the Cappella Sassetti, a cycle of Ghirlandaio frescoes depicting the life of St Francis of Assisi.
☎ 055 21 69 12 ⊠ Piazza di Santa Trinita ☾ 8am-noon & 4-6pm Mon-Sat, 4-6pm Sun & holidays 🚌 6, 11, 36, 37 & A

Chiesa di SS Michele e Gaetano (4, C3)
Even if you're not big on Baroque, the harmonious interior of this rare, intact example of the style is worth a visit (especially if you want to escape the crowds). A church has stood on this site since the 11th century but was completely overhauled in the 17th century according to a design by Buontalenti.
⊠ Via de' Tornabuoni ☾ 1.30-5.30pm 🚌 6, 11, 22, 36, 37 & A

Chiesa e Convento di Santa Maria Maddalena de' Pazzi (7, B2)
The main treat inside this former convent complex (dating from 1257) is not so much the church as what lies beyond it, a remarkable fresco of the crucifixion of Christ done by Pietro Il Perugino in 1493–96. The beauty and freshness of the colours are all the more amazing because they have never been touched by a restorer.
☎ 055 247 84 20 ⊠ Borgo Pinti 58 € €1 ☾ 9am-noon & 5-7pm Mon-Sat 🚌 C

Far from the madding crowds – Chiesa di SS Michele e Gaetano

PIAZZAS & PARKS

Central Florence just doesn't have the sociable, convivial piazzas typical of the rest of the Mediterranean, largely because tourists normally hijack the ones that best suit. However, there are still a few places to rub shoulders with the locals, and each has its own story. The hills backing the Oltrarno are like open country but the bulk of the city north of the Arno is rather less green.

Giardino di Boboli
(4, C9)

The Giardino di Boboli was laid out in a blend of mannerist and Baroque styles in the 16th century as a backyard for Cosimo I and his ailing wife in Palazzo Pitti. Dotted with fountains, ponds and statuary, it is a beautiful green haven in which you will also find the Museo delle Porcellane (p26) and the restored 18th-century Kaffeehaus, perfect for a cuppa (but, at time of writing, is still awaiting the green light to reopen).

☎ 055 265 18 16 ✉ Piazza de' Pitti € €4 includes Museo delle Porcellane & Museo degli Argenti ⏰ 8.15am-5.30pm Mar, 8.15am-6.30pm Apr-May & Sep-Oct, 8.15am-7.30pm Jun-Aug, 8.15am-4.30pm Nov-Feb; closed 1st and last Mon of each month 🚌 D

Piazza del Duomo (4, E3)

This is the holy centre of Florence and was once the site of the town's Roman temple. As the city emerged to become the dominant power in medieval Tuscany, it lavished money and genius on this piazza, a place for Florence to beat its chest proudly and show the world its greatness.
🚌 1, 6, 7, 10, 11, 14, 17, 23 & A

Piazza della Repubblica (4, D4)

In a masterstroke of 19th-century middle-class fatheadedness, this brash, broad and breezy square was ruthlessly gouged out of the ancient city centre (wiping out the Roman forum) during Florence's brief spell as the Italian capital. A huge memorial plaque atop a bombastic triumphal arch proclaims stridently '*l'antico centro della città da secolare squallore a nuova vita restituito*' (the ancient city centre returned to new life after centuries of squalor).
🚌 A

Piazza della Repubblica is full of sweet delights

Piazza della Santissima Annunziata (7, A1)

This elegant and relaxed 16th-century space is flanked on three sides by arcades, including the Brunelleschi-designed and La Robbia-decorated façade of the Spedale degli Innocenti (p28). Commanding from the centre is *Ferdinando I de' Medici*, Giambologna's last statue, finished by his student Pietro Tacca, who also designed the two bizarre Baroque bronze fountains after, perhaps, one too many sleepless nights.
🚌 6, 31, 32 & C

FLORENCE'S GREEN LUNG

There are precious few tracts of green in central Florence (an important one is the Giardino di Boboli, see above). The largest is the Parco delle Cascine (p36), a 3km-long park on the northern bank of the Arno, about 2km west of Ponte Vecchio. A former private hunting ground of the Medici dukes, it was opened to the public in 1776 with boulevards, fountains, bird sanctuaries, playgrounds and a swimming pool.

At the western end of the Parco della Cascine is a monument to Rajaram Cuttiputti, an Indian maharajah who died while holidaying in Florence in 1870 and was cremated by the river, a most extraordinary sight for the Florentines, who named the spot and the nearby bridge after the '*Indiano*'.

Piazza della Signoria
(4, E5)

The city's most splendid piazza has been the hub of Florentine political life since the Middle Ages and is lined with historical buildings and (mostly copies of) famous sculptures. The square itself is something of an art gallery. Ammanati's **Neptune Fountain** dominates the statuary but was a waste of a good block of marble, according to Michelangelo.

🚌 B

Piazza di Santa Croce
(7, A4)

Basilica di Santa Croce keeps haughty watch over this piazza, which was cleared in the Middle Ages to accommodate the overflow from the church. Once the scene of colourful jousts, festivals and the ferocious Calcio Storico (p62), it was also Savonarola's preferred place to execute heretics. Jammed with tourists by day, it's much more pleasant in the evenings when reclaimed by the locals.

🚌 C

THE WORLD TURNS

Galileo Galilei — the founder of modern science, perfector of the telescope and the first person to clearly see that the moon wasn't made of cheese — was born in Pisa in 1564. Although lauded for his discoveries, he got on the wrong side of the ecclesiastical authorities in Rome for defending the theory that, contrary to the scriptures, the earth revolved around the sun. In 1610 he moved to Florence at the invitation of the Medici and lived at Costa di San Giorgio 19 in the Oltrarno for seven years. In 1633, the 71-year-old was hauled before the Inquisition in Rome, charged with heresy and forced to recant his astrological theory. Legend has it that he did so with the aside, *'eppur si muove'* (but it does move). He was then effectively placed under house arrest just outside Florence until his death in 1642. The Vatican cleared him of heresy in 1992.

Piazza di Santa Maria Novella (4, B3)

This vast five-sided piazza was extended several times to accommodate the huge crowds drawn to the Dominican church. From the 16th to the 19th centuries, it hosted the annual Palio dei Cocchi (Chariot Race), which went around the two marble obelisks atop bronze turtles made by Giambologna in 1608. It's a rather dour and uninviting place today but there are ambitious plans to one day remodel the square.

🚌 1, 7, 10, 11, 14, 17, 22, 23, 36, 37 & A

Piazza di Santo Spirito
(3, C7)

Florence's most lively, yet laid-back and local piazza is lined with good cafés and bars spilling out onto the square beneath the façade of Brunelleschi's basilica. It attracts a mixed crowd of students, layabouts, artists, slumming uptowners, savvy foreigners and dodgy hash dealers.

🚌 6 & D

Piazzale Michelangelo
(3, F8)

A few twists and turns above Porta San Niccolò, this affable piazza has a carnival atmosphere at sunset and is the most popular vantage point for views over the city, partly because the car park is big enough to accommodate tour buses.

🚌 12 & 13

Coffee at Rivoire (p60) on Piazza della Signoria

Piazzale Michelangelo (opposite) is a mecca for tourists wanting to view Florence

NOTABLE BUILDINGS

Arte dei Giudici e dei Notai (4, F4)

In a building with Roman foundations and dating to the 14th century, this building was once home to the judges and lawyers' guild. One of the city's premier restaurants, Alle Murate (p52), is lodged beneath wonderfully restored frescoes. By day you can visit the place as a monument, possibly combining with a light lunch. By night you can dine beneath the ceiling frescoes in romantic style.
☎ 055 24 06 18 🖥 www
.artenotai.org ✉ Via del
Proconsolo 16/r € €10
🕐 9am-5pm Tue-Sun
🚌 14, 23 & A

Arte della Lana (4, D4)

The medieval headquarters of the Wool Guild is made up of a tower-house, echoing that very Florentine preoccupation with self-defence

that clearly affected the guilds almost as much as it did feuding families. An eagle clutching a bundle, the guild's symbol, is embossed in stone in several places on the wall on Via Calimaruzza.
✉ Via dell'Arte della
Lana 1 🚌 A

Casa Galleria (3, B6)

An unexpected sight in moody medieval Florence is this Art Nouveau townhouse, built by Giovanni Micheluzzi in 1911 in a rare moment of original 20th-century Florentine architecture. The striking and curvaceous façade is liberally laced with glass and iron, and fronts one of the few buildings of its genre that wasn't pulled down.
✉ Borgo Ognissanti 26
🚌 A

Chiesa Russa Ortodossa (3, D2)

Rising incongruously above the smart *palazzi* north of the centre are five graceful onion domes belonging

to the Russian Orthodox Church, built and decorated by Russian architects and artists in 1902. Florence was a popular 19th-century winter retreat for wealthy Russians – Tchaikovsky and Dostoevsky among them.
☎ 055 49 01 48 ✉ Viale
Giovanni Milton 🕐 3.30pm
service 3rd Sun of month
🚌 4, 8, 13 & 20

Corridoio Vasariano (4, D6-C8)

When Cosimo I moved to Palazzo Pitti in 1564, he got Vasari to build a 1km-long private corridor from the Palazzo Vecchio, through the Uffizi, across the top of Ponte Vecchio, through the Chiesa di Santa Felicita and into their new home. It was a security measure and a means of avoiding the riff-raff. Long home to a collection of secondary art, it is at present closed to the public.
✉ Uffizi to Palazzo Pitti
🚌 B

Take home your very own 'David' from Mercato Nuovo

Forte di Belvedere (3, D8)
Bernardo Buontalenti helped design the rambling fortifications here for Grand Duke Ferdinando I towards the end of the 16th century. The fort makes a wonderful place to stroll, hosts various temporary exhibitions and offers fine views of the city and a terrace bar. It's a 10-minute walk along Costa di San Giorgio from the bus stop.
✉ Costa di San Giorgio
€ €8/5, includes temporary art exhibition ☺ 10am-10pm Wed-Mon, Sep–mid-Jul, 10am-midnight mid-Jul–Aug, exhibition space 10am-7pm Wed-Mon 🚌 D & C

Loggia del Bigallo (4, D3)
This graceful 14th-century marble loggia, opposite the Battistero, was built for the Misericordia charity and served as a lost-and-found office for children; the poor mites who weren't collected within three days were sent on to foster homes. The confraternity has a small museum (p25) across the road behind the ambulances.
✉ Via dei Calzaiuoli 🚌 1, 6, 7, 10, 11, 14, 17, 23 & A

Mercato Nuovo (4, D5)
Built to shelter a market in the 16th century, this handsome loggia was also where medieval Florence's war cart was placed to let locals know trouble was looming. It also contains the Fontana del Porcellino (Piglet's Fountain), Florence's version of the do-this-and-you'll-some-day-return scenario; in this case you must tickle his bum (or rub his nose or something). Dodgy merchants used to be publicly spanked here – check your leather goods carefully or you'll wish they still were.
✉ Via Calimala 🚌 A

Palazzo Antinori (4, B3)
One of Florence's most beautiful 'small' *palazzi*, this golden abode was built in 1465 for Giovanni Boni, a very rich member of the Money Changing Guild, but was taken over by the Antinori wine-making dynasty in the 16th century. Over 100 *palazzi* were built in the 15th century, when mercantile Florence was at its peak.
✉ Piazza Antinori 3 🚌 6, 11, 22, 36, 37 & A

BRIDGE SAGA COMES TO A HEAD

Ponte Santa Trinità (4, B6), undoubtedly the most beautiful bridge in Florence, was designed (probably) by Michelangelo and built by Bartolommeo Amannati in 1567. The statues of the four seasons were added in 1608, and generations admired the elegant crossing until it was blown up by retreating German forces in 1944. Rather than throw some slapdash number back over the river, engineers rebuilt the same bridge, using copies of 16th-century tools and stone from the Boboli quarry. The statues were dredged out of the Arno and the reconstructed bridge was completed in 1958. Well, almost. All that was missing was the head of *Primavera* (Spring). Stories abounded that Allied soldiers made off with it and advertisements were placed in international papers pleading for its return, but to no avail. The city lamented until three years later when municipal divers chanced upon the slightly bashed head, and Florence's most captivating crossing was put back together again.

Primavera (Spring) on Ponte Santa Trinità (opposite)

Palazzo Davanzati (4, C5)
This remarkable 14th-century mansion, nearing completion of a painstaking restoration, is a rare and exquisite example of the medieval mansion of wealthy Florentines. It was purchased in 1904 by Elia Volpi. On view now is probably the most interesting part, the first, or 'noble' floor, whose star is the family dining room or Sala dei Pappagalli (Parrot Hall), so named because of the birds in the fresco décor.
☎ 055 238 86 10 ✉ Via Porta Rossa 13 🕑 8.15am-1.50pm Tue-Sat & alternating Sun & Mon 🚍 A

Palazzo dei Capitani di Parte Guelfa (4, D5)
In the middle of this well-preserved chunk of medieval Florence is the 13th-century 'Palace of the Guelph Faction's Captains', a fortified building raised on land confiscated from the Ghibellines and later touched up by Brunelleschi and Vasari.
✉ Piazza di Parte Guelfa 🚍 A

Palazzo Medici-Riccardi (4, E1)
Cosimo rejected Brunelleschi's design for his new home as too flashy — after which, the furious architect smashed up the model — and plumped instead for Michelozzo's more discreet and refined design. The Riccardi family remodelled the house in the 17th century, but you can still see the Cappella dei Magi, a chapel bursting with the colour of Benozzo Gozzoli's Gothic frescoes depicting the arrival of the Three Wise Men in grand medieval-style procession.
☎ 055 276 03 40 ✉ Via Cavour 4, San Marco € €4 🕑 9am-7pm Thu-Tue 🚍 1, 6, 7, 10, 11 & 17

Palazzo Strozzi (4, C4)
Fifteen buildings were knocked down to make way for this behemoth of golden, rusticated stone, which was built late in the 15th century for the obscenely wealthy Strozzi banking clan. It stayed in the family until 1937, and is now occasionally used as a temporary exhibition space.
✉ Piazza degli Strozzi 🚍 6, 11, 22, 36, 37 & A

Touch Fontana del Porcellino at Mercato Nuovo (opposite) and you are sure to return

FLORENCE FOR CHILDREN

Though you won't see that many of them around – Italy has one of the lowest birth rates in Europe – *bambini* (children) are universally welcomed and pampered by Italians, and you'll rarely have trouble accommodating their 'special needs'. That said, they may get bored with all the Ren, Renai...art and there aren't many specific sights to engage them. Along with the sights listed here, they might enjoy the weird and wonderful curios at the Museo Stibbert (p28), the zoological part of Museo Zoologico La Specola (*not* the gruesome waxed anatomy section; p28), the mummies at the Museo Archeologico (p26), the exotic at the Museo dell'Antropologia e Etnologia (p26) and the antique and pioneering technology of the Museo di Storia della Scienza (p27).

If they need to run off a little energy, send them up the Campanile (p12) or the Duomo's dome (p10). They'll like the open spaces of the Giardino di Boboli (p31) while a dip in a pool (see p84) should soak a sulk. If all this fails, there's no tantrum a face full of *gelati* won't fix.

Giardini d'Azeglio (7, C2)
A rare urban haven, this garden in the shady Piazza d'Azeglio has swings, slides and an old-fashioned merry-go-round. In the late afternoon it fills up with excited children and their wound-up guardians.
✉ Piazza Massimo d'Azeglio 🚌 6, 31 & 32

Mondobimbo (3, F2)
This is a well-stocked playground with everything from bouncy-castles to a minirailway, aimed at kids aged two to 10.
☎ 055 553 29 46 ✉ Via M di Savoia € €5 🕙 10am-1pm & 4-1pm, 10am-7pm Oct-Apr 🚌 13 & 25

Museo dei Ragazzi (4, E6)
Run by the city and based in Palazzo Vecchio, this museum organises activities and educational workshops here and in the Museo di Storia della Scienza and Museo Stibbert. Kids can dress up in period clobber, build models of famous Florentine buildings and discover the mysteries of the bubble.
☎ 055 276 82 24 ✉ Palazzo Vecchio, Piazza della Signoria € per child per activity €8, per family ticket (2 adults & 2/3 children) €21/25 🕙 9am-7pm Fri-Wed, 9am-2pm Thu 🚌 B

Parco delle Cascine (1, C2)
The largest park in the city is dotted with playgrounds and is a great place to let children loose. Families take over on weekends – the park teems with kite-flyers, kids on bikes, bladers and joggers. In summer you can use the

Caricaturist at Piazzo del Duomo

swimming pool **Le Pavoniere** (☎ 055 36 22 33; Viale della Catena 2; €7.50/4.50; 🕙 10am-6pm & 8pm-2am Jun–mid-Sep). Rent bikes from Florence by Bike (p83). ✉ Viale degli Olmi 🚌 1, 9, 12, 13, 16, 26, 27, 80 & B

Piazza de' Ciompi (7, C4)
Named after the textile workers who met to plan their 14th-century revolt, this piazza is best known for its Mercato delle Pulci (Flea Market; p50) and Vasari's graceful 16th-century Loggia del Pesce (Fish Market), which is decorated with terracotta seafood and was moved here when the Mercato Vecchio (Old Market) was torn down. It is also a top spot for mums and dads to take the young kids for squeals of delight on the swings and maybe mucking around with equally contented local little 'uns.
🕙 8.30am-8pm 🚌 C

BABY-SITTING

Almost all of the larger hotels provide child-minding facilities, while most others have arrangements with regular carers or can suggest someone reliable.

Trips & Tours

WALKING TOURS
Introducing Florence

From the museum complex of **Palazzo Pitti** (**1**; p22), head down busy Via de' Guicciardini and onto **Ponte Vecchio** (**2**; p17), Italy's most famous bridge. Notice, overhead to your right, the **Corridoio Vasariano** (**3**; p33), a private walkway built in the 16th century to connect the Medici palaces. Fol-

low it right down Lungarno degli Archibusieri – looking over your shoulder for views of the bridge – and you'll come to the front of the **Uffizi** (**4**; p8), a treasure chest brimming with Renaissance art. Walk between the galleries towards the tower of the **Palazzo Vecchio** (**5**; p20) and emerge onto the open-air sculpture gallery of **Piazza della Signoria** (**6**; p32). Stride through the market stalls lining Via de' Gondi, turning left into Piazza di San Firenze, where you'll face the rather sombre-looking **Bargello** (**7**; p15), containing some of the finest sculptures ever created. Left into Via Dante Alighieri and you'll pass **Casa di Dante** (**8**; p24), the site where the poet supposedly lived. Take a right into Via dei Calzaiuoli, passing **Orsanmichele** (**9**; p29) as you turn. A little way up, remember to keep breathing when the magnificent **Duomo** (**10**; p10) comes into view, flanked by Giotto's **Campanile** (**11**; p12) and facing the doors of the **Battistero** (**12**; p11) that helped launch the Renaissance.

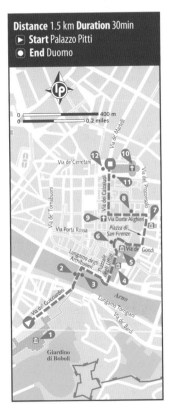

Distance 1.5 km **Duration** 30min
- ▶ **Start** Palazzo Pitti
- ● **End** Duomo

Sellers of beautiful jewellery, buyers, tourists and locals: Ponte Vecchio tempts them all

Bas-relief detail inside Basilica di San Lorenzo

Renaissance Churches

Lunch on Florence's most sociable piazza will launch you into this ecclesiastical jaunt, starting with Brunelleschi's **Basilica di Santo Spirito** (**1**; p29). At the opposite end of the piazza take Via San Agostino right and continue along

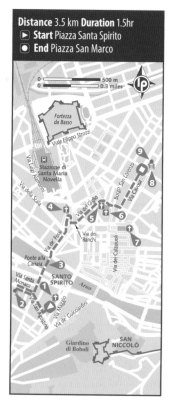

Distance 3.5 km **Duration** 1.5hr
▶ **Start** Piazza Santa Spirito
● **End** Piazza San Marco

Via Santa Monaca. On your left, at the far end of the unremarkable Basilica di Santa Maria del Carmine, is the entrance to the fascinating **Cappella Brancacci** (**2**; p18) with Masaccio's pioneering frescoes. Backtrack to Via de' Serragli, turn left and over the unprepossessing **Ponte alla Carraia** (**3**) and through Via de' Fossi. Across the piazza, you'll spot the fabulous façade of the **Basilica di Santa Maria Novella** (**4**; p23), once the most prestigious church, where rich families vied to create the most impressive chapels. Leave the piazza by Via dei Banchi, turn left at Via del Giglio and you'll arrive at the **Cappelle Medicee** (**5**; p29), the chapels where many of Florence's most famous family are entombed. Next door is the **Basilica di San Lorenzo** (**6**; p16), the Medici's parish church and pet religious project. Following Borgo San Lorenzo south would soon bring you to the **Duomo** (**7**; p10), but head up Via Cavour instead to **Chiesa di San Marco** (**8**) and the **Museo di San Marco** (**9**; p21), dedicated to – and largely decorated by – Fra Angelico.

A Florentine's Florence

Start your leisurely walk on the attractive **Piazza Santissima Annunziata** (**1**; p31), where you'll find cheerful locals, both young and old, passing through or hanging out on the steps of the Brunelleschi-designed **Spedale degli Innocenti** (**2**; p28). The 'hospital of the innocents' was Europe's very first orphanage, founded on the southeast side of the piazza in 1421. Across the road is the **Chiesa della Santissima Annunziata** (**3**), home to Florence's most venerated relic – a 14th-century painting of the Virgin Mary that is unfortunately no longer on display. Legend has it that an angel popped down from the heavens to add the finishing touches. There are also frescoes by Andrea del Castagno, Perugino and Andrea del Sarto. Walk away from the church and turn left into Via degli Alfani, all the way down to the serene **Chiesa di Sant'Ambrogio** (**4**), and turn right onto **Piazza dei Ciompi** (**5**) and a bright little flea market. After your browse, head back to Sant'Ambrogio, turning right into Via de' Macci and then first left to the bustling **Mercato di Sant'Ambrogio** (**6**; p50), one of the best places to peek behind Florence's tourist veil. For lunch, grab a pizza at **Il Pizzaiuolo** (**7**; p56). Wander down Via de' Macci and right on to Via Ghibellina until you come to **Casa Buonarroti** (**8**; p24), essentially a shrine to one of the most famous Florentines, Michelangelo. Take the atmospheric Via delle Pinzochere towards the **Basilica di Santa Croce** (**9**; p19), the Renaissance's pantheon and showcase for some splendid works. **Piazza di Santa Croce** (**10**; p32) is packed with tourists but hums to a local tune in the evenings, when you should return for dinner at **Boccadama** (**11**; p55).

Basicilia di Santa Croce, is known as the Renaissance's pantheon

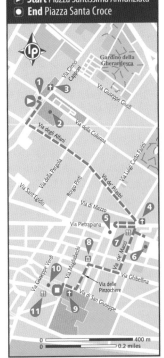

Distance 2.5 km **Duration** 1.5hr
▶ **Start** Piazza Santissima Annunziata
● **End** Piazza Santa Croce

DAY TRIPS
Chianti (2, E3)

Not surprisingly Florence and Siena scrapped for centuries over who would control Chianti. Not only is it one of the world's most famous wine regions, but it's also an area of outstanding natural beauty. The scenery is coffee table–book Tuscan, with castles, villages and villas perched on hilltops sheathed in vines. You can explore by SITA bus but it's much more fun with your own wheels. It starts just 20km south of Florence at **Greve**, the first good base for exploration. Of course, you'll want to take in a visit to a winery but don't leave it to chance as most places require bookings. Ask at the tourist office for information.

INFORMATION
20km south of Florence
- 🚗 follow the signs for the SS222 from Piazza Giuseppe Poggi in Oltrarno
- 🚌 regular SITA buses to Greve from Piazza della Stazione (55min; €2.90)
- ℹ️ tourist office, Viale G da Verrazzano 59; ☎ 055 854 62 87; 9.30am-1.30pm & 2.30-7pm Mon-Sat Mar-Oct
- ✖️ head to Piazza Matteotti in Greve in Chianti (2, E2)

Siena (6)

Indisputably the most beautiful city in the region, Siena is set on three hills and flanked by fertile valleys. It has an enchanting medieval ensemble of turrets and towers. Streets and lanes swirl around the magnificent 14th-century **Campo**, one of Italy's most splendid and sociable piazzas. Twice a year Il Palio, a chaotic bareback horse race around the piazza, is contested by the various *contrade* (districts). Numerous *palazzi*, churches and museums house a giddying volume of art and heritage, and it's impossible to absorb it all in one day.

INFORMATION
70km south of Florence
- 🚗 follow the signs for the SS2 from Porta Romana in the Oltrarno
- 🚌 regular SITA buses from Piazza della Stazione (1¼hr; €6.50)
- 💻 www.terresiena.it
- ℹ️ APT office; Piazza del Campo 56; ☎ 0577 28 05 51; 9am-7pm

Waiting for harvest in a Chianti vineyard

Lucca (2, C1)

While Lucca has been 'discovered', it still gets fewer tourists than other Tuscan towns, and you get the impression that's how the locals like it – tucked in behind their picturesque city walls that look like they were built more for ornamentation than defence. Bicycles are the preferred mode of transport although you could take in the medieval heart on foot in half a day. The dazzling Romanesque church of **San Michele in Foro** has an unforgettable wedding-cake façade while **San Frediano**, around the corner, has a strikingly resplendent mosaic. Narrow streets thread through the town, lined with historical buildings and charming traditional shops. The area is rightly famed for its wonderful selections of olive oil – at locals' prices – so buy up big and enjoy the flavour.

INFORMATION
62km west of Florence
- follow the signs for the A11 to Pisa from Porta al Prato
- regular trains from Stazione di Santa Maria Novella (1½hr; €4.60)
- regular Lazzi buses from Piazza Adua (1¼hr; €4.70)
- www.lucca.turismo.toscana.it
- tourist office; Piazzale Verdi; ☎ 0583 58 31 50; ✆ 9am-7pm Easter-Oct, 9am-5.30pm Nov-Easter

Pisa (5)

Best known for a monumental cock-up, Pisa is the most popular day trip from Florence. Tour buses empty out on to **Campo dei Miracoli** (Field of Miracles), home to a cluster of Italy's most stunning Romanesque gems, the **cathedral** (€2) the **baptistry** (€5) and, of course, the **Leaning Tower** (www.duomo.pisa .it; €17/15 with online booking; ✆ 9am-6pm Mar, 8.30am-8.30pm Apr-Sep, 9am-7pm Oct, 9.30am-5pm Nov-Feb). The crowds head straight for the famed architectural blunder, climb its 293 steps, buy the plastic ornament and retreat to somewhere 'less touristy'. But linger a little and Pisa may charm you. The **Campo Santo** (cemetery), is said to contain soil brought back from Calvary during the Crusades. Pisa's complex opening hours change regularly, so check them on the spot.

INFORMATION
81km west of Florence
- follow the signs for the A11 to Pisa from Porta al Prato
- regular trains from Stazione di Santa Maria Novella (1hr 5min; €4.85)
- www.pisa.turismo.toscana.it (in Italian)
- APT office; Via Pietro Nenni 24; ☎ 050 56 04 64; ✆ 9am-7pm Mon-Sat, 10.30am-4.30pm Sun Apr-Oct; 9am-6pm Mon-Sat, 10.30am-4.30pm Sun Nov-Mar

FORZA FIESOLE

Nestled in the hilly valleys 8km north of Florence, ancient Fiesole offers atmospheric and winding streets, fresh air, spectacular views back to the city and a smattering of sights, including a Duomo, a reasonable art museum and an impressive architectural site with Roman theatre. Take bus 7 from Stazione di Santa Maria Novella.

ORGANISED TOURS

You can arrange a personal guide with, among others, the **Associazione Guide Turistiche Toscane** (☎ 055 264 52 17; www .florencetouristguides.com) and the **Associazione Centro Guide Turismo** (☎ 055 28 84 48).

Associazione Mercurio (4, E1)

There's so much art in Florence that the Renaissance can sometimes feel like an impenetrable wall, especially the Uffizi and Galleria dell'Accademia. This company specialises in two- to three-hour tours through the museums, led by lecturers and art historians.

☎ 055 21 33 55 ⌨ www .mercurio-italy.org ✉ c/- Amici del Turismo Travel Agency, Via Cavour 36/r € €40 ⏲ 9am-1pm & 2-6pm Mon-Fri

CAF Tours (4, B1)

This long-established Italian company offers a variety of one-day tours of the city (by foot and by coach) and beyond, including to Siena, San Gimignano and even to Rome and Orvieto. The city tours take place by day and night and can include guided museum visits. Groups can be big and are generally pretty conservative.

☎ 055 21 06 12 ⌨ www .caftours.com ✉ Via Sant'Antonino 6/r € €24-69

Comune di Firenze tourist office (4, A1)

The tourist office puts on a series of tours for small groups (in Italian). You can get the latest programme and booking details from the tourist offices. The city hall also promotes a series of thematic walking tours, the Percorsi Culturali Firenze e il Novecento (☎ 055 262 59 55; www.comune.firenze .it/firenze900).

☎ 055 21 22 45 ⌨ www .comune.firenze.it ✉ Piazza della Stazione 4

Florence by Bike (3, D3)

If you've got energy to burn and a hardy backside, take this invigorating 35km day-ride into Chianti country, where you can enjoy splendid Tuscan views. Groups do not exceed 10 people and tours include lunch and a little wine-tasting.

☎ 055 48 89 92 ⌨ www .florencebybike.it ✉ Via San Zanobi 120-122/r € €68

I Bike Italy

'No churches, no museums, no annoying crowds' is the promise of this outfit, which offers excellent single- and two-day cycle tours around Fiesole, the Chianti and down to Siena. They organise shuttle buses to and from Florence and their base north of the city.

☎ 055 234 23 71 ⌨ www .ibikeitaly.com € 1-/2-day ride US$85/280

Walking Tours of Florence (4, D6)

Florence's biggest specialist walking company organises a range of two- to three-hour walks — with up to 30 people — around the city and beyond, led by bubbly American art-history graduates. You can also organise private tours and jaunts elsewhere in Tuscany.

☎ 055 264 50 33 ⌨ www .artviva.com ✉ Piazza de'Santo Stefano 2 € €25-39 ⏲ 8am-6.30pm Mon-Sat, 9am-noon Sun

Terravision City Sightseeing Bus (4, B1)

With a 24-hour pass (adult/ child aged six to 15 €20/10) you have unlimited use of two hop-on-hop-off circle-line tourist bus lines around the city and to/from Fiesole. Line A comes every 20 to 30 minutes (9am to 6.30pm, hourly 7pm to 11pm), while Line B does a longer route to Fiesole and back. You can pick up either bus just outside the main train station or at any stop along the way.

Cyclists traverse the historic streets

Shopping

For many, doing the Duomo is little more than a pretext for coming to Florence and hitting the shops. The city has been synonymous with style and fine craftsmanship since medieval times, when goldsmiths, tailors and shoemakers got the same kudos as sculptors and artists. If you're in the market for classic fashion, leather, jewellery, silverwork, stationery, food or wine, buy some extra luggage to take the goodies home!

Shopping Areas

The medieval core is mainly dedicated to fashion, with the streets of **Via de' Tornabuoni** and **Via della Vigna Nuova** the altar of *haute couture*. **Borgo San Lorenzo** is where many Florentines head for shoes, while **Santa Croce** is the heart of leather land. **Borgo Ognissanti**, **Via de' Fossi** and **Via Maggio** are the antique strips, while the whole of the **Oltrarno** abounds with traditional artisans' shops and studios, temples to handmade good taste.

Italian leather: Italian Style with a capital S!

LEGENDARY LABELS

Emilio Pucci (4, C5)
Most famous for its 1960s bold and bright-coloured psychedelic prints, Pucci relaunched its vintage line in the early 90s and were copied by just about every high-street label on the planet. Swimwear, beach towels, bags and shoes are available in distinctive Pucci style.
☎ 055 29 40 28 ⊠ Via de' Tornabuoni 20-22 ⏱ 3.30-7.30pm Mon, 10am-1pm & 3.30-7.30pm Tue-Sat 🚌 6, 11, 22, 36, 37 & A

Ermanno Scervino (4, C3)
Scervino appeals to the young set conscious of the

Gucci has many followers...

latest moves on the threads front, which often means a walk on the grunge side.
☎ 055 260 87 14
⊠ Piazza degli Antinori 10/r ⏱ 10am-7.30pm Mon-Sat 🚌 6 & A

Gucci (4, C4)
Gucci first made its name with luggage and leather accessories created in a tiny saddlery store around the corner from here, and is now the world's best-known Florentine trademark. Thanks to family feuding there are no Guccis left in the business but the name still excites aficionados.
☎ 055 26 40 11 🖥 www .gucci.com ⊠ Via de' Tornabuoni 73/r ⏱ 3-7pm Mon, 10am-7pm Tue-Sat 🚌 6, 11, 22, 36, 37 & A

Prada (4, C4)
This century-old family business is best known for its simplicity in design and colour as well as the distinctive red stripe on the back heel of its shoes. Cutting-edge silhouettes and fabrics adopted by design junkies.
☎ 055 28 34 39 🖥 www .prada.it ⊠ Via de' Tornabuoni 51/r ⏱ 10am-7pm Mon-Sat 🚌 6, 11, 22, 36, 37 & A

Roberto Cavalli (4, C4)
Cavalli is riding a fashion-world wave with his rock-and-roll wardrobe. This is real-impact statement fashion with wild and wonderful creations from shoes and underwear to over-the-top overcoats.
☎ 055 239 62 26 🖥 www .robertocavalli.net ⊠ Via de' Tornabuoni 83/r ⏱ 3-7.30pm Sun-Mon, 10am-7.30pm Tue-Sat 🚌 6, 11, 22, 36, 37 & A

OUTLETS FOR YOUR OBSESSION

Label lovers on the hunt for a bargain should visit the designer-outlet stores southeast of Florence, where you can get up to 60% off previous seasons' collections. For general information look up www.outlet-firenze.com.

The biggest is **The Mall** (2, F2; ☎ 055 865 77 75; Via Europa 8, Leccio Reggello; ⏱ 10am-7pm Mon-Sat, 3-7pm Sun), where Gucci leads the way. Also represented here are Agnona, Ermenegildo Zegna, Tod's, Yves Saint Laurent, Sergio Rossi, Armani, Ferragamo, Valentino, Loro Piana and Bottega Veneta. The Mall runs a daily shuttle from Florence (€25 return) – call to book. A public bus service (each way €2.60; 9am & 12.30pm, Mon-Fri, 9am Sat) runs from the SITA bus station (3, B5), returning at noon and 5pm.

Other outlets in the area include **Dolce & Gabbana** (2, F2; ☎ 055 833 13 00; Località Santa Maria Maddalena, Via Piana dell'Isola 49, Rignano sull'Arno; ⏱ 9am-7pm Mon-Sat, 3-7pm Sun) and **Prada** (2, F3; ☎ 055 9 19 01; Località Levanella, Montevarchi; ⏱ 9.30am-7pm Mon-Sat, 3-7pm Sun).

In Florence you'll find some 'stockhouses' selling discounted and discontinued lines from big labels. Try **Stockhouse Il Giglio** (3, B5; ☎ 055 21 75 96; Borgo Ognissanti 86/r; bus A).

THE HIGH PRICE OF FAKING IT

An adrenaline rush for the lady who loves to shop – and doesn't want to pay retail – is a purchase from the not-so-clandestine hawkers selling fake designer bags around Ponte Vecchio and the Duomo. Haggle like crazy and you can get excellent rip-offs for a fraction of their normal cost. The blood rush is accentuated by the knowledge that, if you are caught in the act by the constabulary, you face a fine of €3300 to €10,000!

BOUTIQUES & LOCAL DESIGNERS

Luisa (4, D3)

This *alta moda* boutique, a Florentine institution, is a one-stop shop for many of the world's top designers. It has its own small line and the haughtiest sales assistants in Florence.

☎ 055 21 78 26 ☐ www .luisaviaroma.com ✉ Via Roma 19-21/r ⏲ 10am-7.30pm Mon-Fri, 10am-2pm Sat 🚌 A

Patrizia Pepe (4, D3)

This husband-and-wife team from nearby Prato put a contemporary spin on classic motifs to come up with *uber*-sexy clothing perfect for the elegant girl-about-town.

☎ 055 264 50 56 ☐ www.patriziapepe.com ✉ Piazza di San Giovanni 12/r ⏲ 10am-7pm Mon-Fri, 10am-2pm Sat 🚌 1, 6, 7, 10, 11, 14, 17, 23 & A

LEATHER

Your feet will itch to try on splendid shoes in Florence. The city has an established name for leather, from world-class to rubbish. When in the markets, especially the San Lorenzo stalls, haggle like hell and examine every stitch. Indeed, make it a rule always to have a good look before purchasing. These shops guarantee quality without the buzz of bargaining.

Bojola (4, C3)

Classic belts, wallets and luggage are offered at this venerable establishment, one of Florence's top shops for hide, where the same family have been turning out quality items for more than a century.

☎ 055 21 11 55 ☐ www .bojola.it ✉ Via de' Rondinelli 25/r ⏲ 9.30am-7pm Mon-Sat 🚌 6, 11, 22, 36, 37 & A

Francesco da Firenze (3, B6)

Come and do your shoes the way they used to be done. Buy ready-made or have them specifically designed. Either way they are hand-made in this topsy-turvy workshop.

☎ 055 21 24 28 ✉ Via di Santo Spirito 62/r ⏲ 9.30am-1pm & 3.30-7.30pm Mon-Fri, 9.30am-1pm Sat 🚌 D

Il Bisonte (4, B5)

Quality craftsmanship is a byword at 'The Bison', particularly accessories that range from elegant bags in natural leather to distinguished desktop items, leather-bound notebooks, briefcases and the like.

☎ 055 21 57 22 ✉ Via del Parione 31/r ⏲ 3.30-7.30pm Mon, 10am-1pm & 3.30-7.30pm Tue-Sat 🚌 A

Madova (4, C7)

If it's quality leather gloves you're after, you won't find a better selection or service than at this old favourite.

☎ 055 239 65 26 ☐ www .madova.com ✉ Via de' Guicciardini 1/r ⏲ 9.30am-7.30pm Mon-Sat 🚌 D

Peruzzi (7, A4)

A huge emporium containing all the things you can make from animal hide, this shop also sells designer clothing and accessories, has an alterations service and can personalise your purchases.

Leather coats are traffic stoppers on Via Faenza

☎ 055 28 90 39 ⌨ www
.peruzzispa.com ✉ Borgo
de' Greci 8-22/r ⊗ 9am-7pm
Mon-Sat 🚌 14, 23 & A

Salvatore Ferragamo
(4, B5)
Another grand Florentine
name – which takes up
an entire block, so is virtually
impossible to miss –
Ferragamo gained fame by
custom making shoes for
famous feet – think Kather-
ine Hepburn. Men can order
made-to-measure shoes
and choose the material,
from crocodile skin to classic
leather. The boutique also
turns out clothes and accessories for the more mature
and conservative fashion fol-
lower. There is a curious shoe
museum too (see p27).
☎ 055 29 21 23 ⌨ www
.salvatoreferragamo.it
✉ Via de' Tornabuoni 16/r
⊗ 10am-7.30pm Mon-Sat
🚌 6, 11, 36, 37 & A

Scuola del Cuoio (7, B5)
If you're hell-bent on
leather, you'll get a good
idea of quality-price ratios
at this guild (in the cloisters

of Basilica di Santa Croce)
where apprentices beaver
away producing high-
quality, old-fashioned
products that you can even
have stamped with your
own mark.
☎ 055 24 45 33 ⌨ www
.leatherschool.it ✉ Piazza
Santa Croce 16 ⊗ 10am-
1pm & 3.30-7pm Mon-Sat
🚌 C

Sergio Rossi (4, D3)
Pop into what feels like
Sergio's very own living
room where, elegantly
strewn about, you'll find
some of his supersexy shoes
for women – stilettos reign
supreme. While steeped in
the classic, his creations are

innovative in colour and
design.
☎ 055 29 48 73 ✉ Via
Roma 15 ⊗ 3-7pm Mon,
10am-7pm Tue-Sat 🚌 A

Tod's (4, C4)
The quintessential Italian
shoe merchants have been
dressing the heels of Florentine families for decades.
Tod's classic, comfy loafers,
in all manner of shapes, sizes
and colours, are best known
for the practical rubber studs
on their heels, which help
reduce driving scuffs.
☎ 055 21 94 23 ✉ Via de'
Tornabuoni 103/r, Medieval
Core ⊗ 10am-7pm Mon-Fri,
10am-2pm Sat 🚌 6, 11, 22,
36, 37 & A

Displayed behind glass, leather becomes works of art

JEWELLERY

Alessandro Dari (7, A6)
One of the key names on the city's jewellery scene today, this master craftsman turns out remarkable castellated rings and at times some rather over-the-top pieces of jewellery.
☎ 055 24 47 47 ⊠ Via San Niccolò 115/r 🕑 9.30am-1.30pm & 4-7.30pm Mon-Sat 🚌 12, 13, 23 & C

Bulgari (4, D3)
Italy's most prestigious jeweller is famous for large colourful stones in antique and slick modern settings. It also has a huge range of products from watches to perfume. It's set out like a museum.
☎ 055 239 67 86 🖳 www .bulgari.com ⊠ Via de' Tornabuoni 61/r 🕑 10am-7pm Tue-Fri 🚌 6, 11, 22, 36, 37 & A

Gherardi (4, D6)
One of the name jewellers on the bridge, Gherardi is without doubt Florence's king of coral and has a chest full of finely crafted treasures from clumps of gold to sought after cultured pearls.
☎ 055 28 72 11 ⊠ Ponte Vecchio 8/r 🕑 9am-7pm Mon-Sat 🚌 B, C & D

Il Gatto Bianco (4, D6)
Fresh and contemporary designs in a range of silver, gold, precious and semi-precious stones are available from this studio.
☎ 055 28 29 89
⊠ Borgo Santi Apostoli 12/r 🕑 10am-1.30pm & 3-7.30pm Mon-Sat 🚌 B

FOOD & DRINK

Enoteche (wine shops) and *alimentari* (grocery stores-cum-delicatessens) abound throughout the city, many offering a little bit of everything.

Dolceforte (4, A2)
This place sells exquisite chocolates, including sweet Duomos, Davids and Ponte Vecchios. The perishable cocoa confections are replaced with equally delectable preserves and jams in summer.
☎ 055 21 91 16 ⊠ Via della Scala 21 🕑 10am-1pm & 4-8pm Mon-Sat 🚌 11, 36, 37 & A

Enoteca Romano Gambi (4, C6)
This traditional shop has quality food and wines from Tuscany and beyond, dispensed by friendly and helpful staff.
☎ 055 29 26 46 ⊠ Borgo Santi Apostoli 21-23/r

🕑 2.30-7.30pm Mon, 10am-7.30pm Tue-Sat 🚌 B

La Galleria del Chianti (4, E4)
Despite the name, the shelves of this store are stacked with goodies from all over Tuscany and even a few from other regions, such as Poli Grappa from Bassano del Grappa in the Veneto (that's if your insides need a clean).
☎ 055 29 14 40 ⊠ Via del Corso 41/r 🕑 9am-8.30pm Mon-Fri, 10am-8.30pm Sat & Sun 🚌 A

Pegna (4, E4)
A good selection of Tuscan and regional Italian specialities such as pâté, cheese, coffees, preserves and other stuff too good to be called just groceries can be found in this mini-supermarket.
☎ 055 28 27 01 ⊠ Via dello Studio 26/r 🕑 9am-1pm & 3.30-7.30pm Mon-Sat 🚌 A

ART GALLERIES

Biagiotti (4, B3)
This stunningly converted 15th-century *palazzo* exhibits the works of many of Italy's most gifted and innovative upcoming artists.
☎ 055 29 42 65 ✉ Via delle Belle Donne 39/r 🕙 2-7pm Mon-Fri 🚌 A

Brancolini Grimaldi (4, D6)
Part of the Ferragamo corporation, this gallery exhibits new and established artists (some local but mostly foreign), and is particularly strong in photography.
☎ 055 28 15 49 🖥 www .isabellabrancolini.it ✉ Vicolo dell'Oro 2/r 🕙 10am-1pm & 3-7pm Mon-Sat 🚌 B

Galleria Tornabuoni (4, C4)
The city's most prestigious gallery presents the works of some of the best and most well-known Italian contemporary artists.
☎ 055 28 47 20 ✉ Via de' Tornabuoni 74/r 🕙 9.30am-1pm & 3.30-7.30pm Mon-Sat 🚌 6, 11, 22, 36, 37 & A

Galleria Tornabuoni

BOOKS & MUSIC

BM Bookshop (3, C6)
Here you'll find a fair spread of volumes on Florence and Tuscany, as well as speciality books on art and fiction, plus a huge selection of Italian cookbooks in English.
☎ 055 29 45 75 ✉ Borgo Ognissanti 4/r 🕙 9.30am-7.30pm Mon-Sat 🚌 A

Data Records (7, A5)
It prides itself on finding all sorts of obscure stuff, in CD and vinyl, which would be quite a job considering the sheer volume of records stacked up here in seemingly arbitrary fashion. There's a big bargain section and rarities can be found out the back.
☎ 055 28 75 92 ✉ Via dei Neri 15/r 🕙 4-8pm Mon, 10am-1pm & 4-8pm Tue-Sat 🚌 13, 23, B & C

Edison (4, D4)
A super bookstore in central Florence, Edison has a relaxed coffee shop, Internet access and video screens showing satellite news. There's an excellent English-language travel section.
☎ 055 21 31 10 🖥 www .libreriaedison.it ✉ Piazza della Repubblica 27/r 🕙 9am-midnight Mon-Sat, 10am-midnight Sun 🚌 A

McRae Books (7, A5)
A well-stocked English-language bookshop a stone's throw from Piazza della Signoria. Apart from the impressive range of reading material, it has the advantage of opening Sundays.
☎ 055 238 24 56 🖥 www .mcraebooks.com ✉ Via de' Neri 32/r 🕙 9am-7.30pm 🚌 B

Paperback Exchange (7, B3)
A vast collection of new and secondhand English-language books can be found here, including classics, contemporary literature, reference books, bestsellers and travel guides, as well as titles on the Renaissance and its major players.
☎ 055 247 81 54 🖥 www .papex.it ✉ Via Fiesolana 31/r 🕙 9am-7.30pm Mon-Fri, 10am-1pm & 3.30-7.30pm Sat 🚌 C

Ricordi Mediastore (4, D4)
A reliable media store with jazz and classical downstairs, rock and pap (not a typo) in the middle, plus instruments and a huge range of sheet music and scores upstairs.
☎ 055 21 41 04 ✉ Via Brunelleschi 8/r 🕙 3.30-7.30pm Mon, 9.30am-7.30pm Tue-Sat 🚌 A

DEPARTMENT STORES

COIN (4, E4)

Good as far as department stores go, this is a stylish, multifloored display case for midrange, middle-class fashion and accessories at reasonable prices.

☎ 055 28 05 31 ⊠ Via dei Calzaiuoli 56/r ⏱ 9.30am-8pm Mon-Sat, 11am-8pm Sun 🚌 A

La Rinascente (4, D4)

A modest branch of the famous national chain, the six floors of this place are a monument to conservatism – everything from Tuscan handicrafts to designer labels and jewellery.

☎ 055 239 85 44 🖥 www .rinascente.it ⊠ Piazza della Repubblica 1 ⏱ 9am-9pm Mon-Sat, 10.30am-8pm Sun 🚌 A

FOR CHILDREN

Assunta Anichini (4, A4)
Founded in 1912, this is the oldest children's clothing shop in Florence. The styles of their exquisite suits and dresses have changed little since – all the clothes are still made by hand and with the best fabrics.

☎ 055 28 49 77 🖥 www .anichini.net ⊠ Via del Parione 59/r ⏱ 3.30-7.30pm Mon, 9am-1pm & 3.30-7.30pm Tue-Sat 🚌 A & B

Bartolucci (4, E5)

The Bartolucci clan use pine to create a remarkable range of toys, models and trinkets that may appeal as much to you as your little 'un.

☎ 055 21 17 73 🖥 www .bartolucci.com ⊠ Via della

Not all shopping is 'adults only' – everyone loves toys

Condotta 12/r ⏱ 3.30-7.30pm Mon, 9am-7.30pm Tue-Sat 🚌 A

Dreoni (4, E1)

Florence's leading toy store is full of fun stuff for kids and also has models that seem to attract just as many adults (well, blokes).

☎ 055 21 66 11 ⊠ Via Cavour 33/r ⏱ 9am-1pm & 3.30-7.30pm Mon-Fri, 9am-1pm Sat 🚌 1, 6, 7, 10, 11, 14, 17, 23 & A

Loretta Caponi (4, C3)

Mums – and just about anyone who likes their home comforts – will lose their minds in this adorable store and atelier, where nimble fingers produce some of the most exquisitely fine and stylish household linens, children's clothing, towels and tablecloths you'll ever purchase.

☎ 055 21 36 68 ⊠ Piazza degli Antinori 4/r ⏱ 9am-1pm & 3.30-7.30pm Mon-Fri, 9am-1pm Sat 🚌 6, 11, 22, 36, 37 & A

SPECIALIST SHOPS

Bartolini (4, F2)

If you're smitten with Italian food and packing your bags with Italian cookbooks, save

some room for the goodies in here: everything you need for the Italian kitchen, from polenta-stirring spoons to artisan ceramics.

☎ 055 21 18 95 ⊠ Via dei Servi 30/r ⏱ 3.30-7pm Mon, 9.30am-12.30pm & 3.30-7pm Tue-Sat 🚌 C

Chebà (4, E5)

For a light and sunny Tuscan slant on ceramics, pop in for colourful plates of poppies or grapevine-decorated saucers. Hand-painted pottery with cheery country and, in some cases, impressionist scenes.

☎ 055 28 18 55 ⊠ Via de' Cerchi 8/r, Medieval Core ⏱ 10.30am-7.30pm Mon-Sat 🚌 A

Luca della Robbia (4, F5)

This shop has been turning out handmade reproductions of *robbiane* (Renaissance-style glazed terracotta) since the 19th century.

☎ 055 28 35 32 ⊠ Via del Proconsolo 19/r ⏱ 10am-6.30pm 🚌 14, 23 & A

Officina Profumo Farmaceutica di Santa Maria Novella (4, A2)

This ancient Dominican apothecary is one of the world's oldest pharmacies.

Ornately decorated and heavenly scented rooms are stocked with emollients, perfumes and herbal medicines designed to fix anything from tired eyes to cellulite.
☎ 055 21 62 76 ⊠ Via della Scala 16 ⏰ 9.30am-7.30pm Mon-Sat 🚍 11, 36, 37 & A

Parione (4, B5)
Established in 1923, this stationery shop gives you a real sense of the long tradition of this cherished Florentine craft. You can expect to see adorable minature bookshelves, puppet models, cards of every description, as well as beautifully bound books and other paper products.
☎ 055 21 56 84 ⊠ Via del Parione 10/r ⏰ 9am-1pm & 3-7.30pm Mon-Sat 🚍 A & B

Pineider (4, D5)
Italy's most exclusive stationer began business here in 1774 and once designed calling cards for the likes of Napoleon. You can get their elegant writing paper, stationery and other materials in branches around the world but it all still starts here.
☎ 055 21 16 05 ⊠ Piazza della Signoria 13/r ⏰ 3.30-7.30pm Sun-Mon, 10am-2pm & 3.30-7.30pm Tue-Sat 🚍 B

Vannucchi (4, E5)
Via della Condotta was long known as the paper-vendors' street in Florence, and at this historic shop they know a thing or two about the business. Apart from quality writing materials (pens and other accessories) you can splash out on high-quality gift-wrapping paper, stationery and *carta fiorentina* (Florentine paper, with floral motifs).
☎ 055216752 ⊠ Via della Condotta 26-28/r, Medieval Core ⏰ 10am-7pm Mon-Sat 🚍 A

TO MARKET, TO MARKET

Shoppers will be drawn to the bustle of the Florence's produce markets and the hope of bargains in the leather *souqs*. You can browse a couple of curious curio collections too.

- **Mercato Centrale** (4, C1; Piazza del Mercato Centrale; ⏰ 7am-2pm Mon-Fri, 7am-2pm & 4-8pm Sat; bus 4, 11, 12, 25, 31, 32 & 33) The city's main produce market, built in the 19th century and bursting with goodies.
- **Mercato delle Cascine** (1, D2; Viale Abramo Lincoln; ⏰ 8am-noon Tue; bus B) Florence's only all-in-one market sets up in Le Cascine on Tuesdays.
- **Mercato delle Pulci** (7, C4; Piazza dei Ciompi ⏰ 10am-7pm Thu-Sun; bus A & C) The only genuine, sift-through-the-crap-and-find-the-goodies flea market in Florence.
- **Mercato Nuovo** (4, D5; Loggia Mercato Nuovo ⏰ 8am-7pm Tue-Sat; bus A) For tourist kitsch and leather.
- **Mercato di San Lorenzo** (4, C1; Via dell'Ariento & around ⏰ 9am-7.30pm Tue-Sat; bus 4, 11, 12, 25, 31, 32 & 33) A boisterous street leather market around the Mercato Centrale.
- **Mercato di Sant'Ambrogio** (7, C4; Piazza Ghiberti; ⏰ 8am-2pm Mon-Sat; bus C) A chirpy produce market.

A bevvy of belts at Mercato di San Lorenzo

Eating

Tuscan cuisine, simple but temptingly hearty fare, will have you drooling but be aware that many places in Florence's historic centre are monumentally mediocre and outrageously overpriced. Choose carefully.

Most popular is the trattoria, casual, family-fun places that serve traditional food. An *osteria* is often similar but traditionally more of a tavern with food and drinks, while an *enoteca* (wine house) specialises in wine by the glass and offers anything from snacks to substantial meals. A *ristorante* is, theoretically at least, a more elaborate affair. The pizzeria needs no introduction.

Bills generally include *pane e coperto* (basically, a cover charge), ranging from €1 to €5 per person. Service may or not be added. If not, 10% is typical although Italy does not have a great tipping culture and anything you leave is discretionary.

Eating in Florence

Colazione (breakfast) is generally no more than a quick *cornetto* (croissant) and coffee at a bar on the way to work. *Pranzo* (lunch) is traditionally the main meal, taken between 12.30pm and 2.30pm, and can start with the antipasto (starter), followed by a *primo,* usually pasta or risotto, and a *secondo,* generally of meat or fish accompanied by a *contorno* (vegetable side dish, which you may or may not have to order separately). Bringing

QUANTO COSTA?

The pricing symbols used in this chapter indicate the cost of a three-course meal (*primo, secondo* and *dolce*) à la carte, and including house wine. Where such a meal is unlikely – in a pizzeria, café or pastry shop – use the symbols as general guidelines only.

€€€€	over €50
€€€	€36–50
€€	€21–35
€	under €20

up the rear is the *dolce* (dessert), *formaggio* (cheese) or *frutta* (fruit) and coffee. *Cena* (dinner) is traditionally a simpler affair along the same lines and eaten between 7.30pm and 10pm.

Do truffle dogs eat olives?

MEDIEVAL CORE

Alle Murate (4, F4)
Modern Italian €€€€
A must for visiting foodies, this elegant and discreet restaurant, which moved home in mid-2005, combines the best of contemporary Italian cooking with a monumental wine list featuring labels from throughout Italy and a few from France. Dine under the exquisite medieval frescoes, among them the earliest known portrait of Dante. See also the Arte dei Giudici e Notai (p33).
☎ 055 24 06 18 🖳 www .artenotai.org ✉ Via del Proconsolo 16/r ⏲ dinner only Tue-Sun 🚌 14, 23 & A Ⓥ

Caffè Coquinarius (4, E4)
Wine Bar €€
An excellent choice outside rigid meal times, this laid-back and comfy café in a former stables has light and substantial dishes of *crostini,* salads, pastas and the usual meaty mains as well as more than a dozen wines by the glass.
☎ 055 230 21 53 ✉ Via delle Oche 15/r ⏲ 9am-midnight, kitchen open noon-11pm 🚌 A ♿ Ⓥ

Frescobaldi (4, E5)
Modern Tuscan & Wine Bar €€
The wine bar (run by one of Tuscany's name wine dynasties) spills out into a lovely courtyard where you can enjoy nibbles and superb wines by the glass. The restaurant is decked out in garish patterns and is less cosy, but the terrific seasonal and Tuscan fare will take your mind off it (if the wine doesn't first).
☎ 055 28 47 24 ✉ Via dei Magazzini 2-4/r ⏲ lunch & dinner Tue-Sat, dinner only Sun-Mon 🚌 A Ⓥ

Gustavino (4, E5)
Italian & Wine Bar €€€
This is a place to be seen, literally, from the street! A fresh, crisp modern air pervades with the metal-and-glass dominated décor. Regional dishes are given unexpected twists and you can select from an extensive range of local wines.
☎ 055 239 98 06 🖳 www .gustavino.it ✉ Via della Condotta 37/r ⏲ lunch & dinner Tue-Sun 🚌 A

THE TUSCAN TABLE

Tuscan gastronomy is steeped in peasant traditions and bursts with the flavour of fresh ingredients, cooked simply and healthily to produce meals rich in flavour and texture.

Classic Tuscan *antipasti* (often served as *aperitivi* in bars) are *crostini,* lightly grilled slices of bread covered in anything from chicken-liver pâté to diced tomato.

Some pasta dishes figure as *primi,* such as ravioli (filled with spinach and ricotta) topped with *burro e salvia* (butter and sage), or *pappardelle* (broad ribbon pasta) with game meats such as *lepre* (hare), *cinghiale* (wild boar) or duck. Tuscan tradition, however, largely ignored pasta in favour of such dishes as the tomato-and-bread mush known as *pappa al pomodoro,* and ribollita (a reboiled bean and vegetable soup flavoured with black cabbage). *Panzanella* (stale, soaked bread with mixed salad, herbs and oil) is a delicious summery starter.

Of the *secondi,* meat is preferred and the *bistecca alla fiorentina* (a thick, succulent T-bone steak grilled over coals) is king (and back on the menus after years on the EU black list because of mad-cow scares). The best, locals reckon, is Chianina meat from herds run in southern Tuscany.

The classic Tuscan dessert is almond-based *cantucci* (biscuits made especially in Siena), accompanied by sweet *vin santo* (the local dessert wine).

Oliviero (4, C5)
Modern Italian €€€€
Red velvet banquettes, pink candles and salmon tablecloths lend this place a jaded dolce-vita air although there's nothing tired about the creative Italian fare and impeccable service. This is a great spot for indulgence or a kookily romantic *cena a due*. ☎ 055 28 76 43 🖳 www.ristorante-oliviero.it ✉ Via delle Terme 51/r 🕒 dinner only Mon-Sat 🚌 B **V**

Perché No (4, E4)
Gelateria €
You'll find wonderful *gelati* and friendly service in this legendary 1930s shop. Creamy chocolates, caramels and coffees compete for your attention with tangy summer fruit numbers. ☎ 055 239 89 69 ✉ Via del Tavolini 19/r 🕒 10.30am-midnight Wed-Sun 🚌 A 👶

Procacci (4, C4)
Café €€
Truffles – particularly *panini tartufati* (tiny sandwiches with truffle pâté) – are the speciality in this divine shop that time appears to have left behind. Wash these tasty morsels down with a glass of *prosecco* (a sparkling white wine) and don't let the off-hand staff spoil the moment. ☎ 055 21 16 56 ✉ Via de' Tornabuoni 64/r 🕒 lunch & dinner Tue-Sat 🚌 6, 11, 22, 36, 37 & A **V**

Ristorante Self-Service Leonardo (4, C3)
Italian €
It's got all the atmosphere of a factory canteen – offset by the chatty old gents who

Rustic Tuscan is on the menu at Vini e Vecchi Sapori

run it – but this large, overly bright self-service joint will do for an uncomplicated feast of salads, fruits and hot dishes courtesy of *bain marie*. ☎ 055 28 44 46 ✉ Via de' Pecori 35/r 🕒 lunch & dinner Sun-Fri 🚌 A 👶 **V**

Vini e Vecchi Sapori (4, E5)
Osteria €
The charmingly miserable owner of this culinary cubby hole stands among diners giving the impression that the background opera is the soundtrack to his life. The bar is laden with delicious antipasto, the menu is full of rustic Tuscan specialities – the *fagiolotti* with pear and *pecorino* is sensational – while the communal wine flows freely between tables. ☎ 055 29 30 45 ✉ Via dei Magazzini 3/r 🕒 1-11pm Tue-Sat, lunch only Sun 🚌 A 👶 **V**

SAN LORENZO & SAN MARCO

Caffellatte (7, B2)
Café €
The name says it all, and this teeny-weeny spot is a great place to linger over a bowlful of velvety coffee. Caffellatte has been supplying the neighbourhood with milky delights for nearly a century, and also has an organic bakery and healthy, light lunches. ☎ 055 247 88 78 ✉ Via degli Alfani 39/r 🕒 8am-midnight Mon-Sat 🚌 C 👶 **V**

Da Nerbone (3, D4)
Market Restaurant €
In the far left corner of the Mercato Centrale (as you enter from the piazza), Nerbone is your classic frills-free market stall/eatery where budget tourists, hurried locals, market workers and

DINING DILEMMAS

Having trouble deciding where to dine? The following may provide the solution.

Deals & Dinners

If you're in town for business, you will make an impression at Ristorante Beccofino (p59) and Alle Murate (p52), and some of the increasingly trendy hotel restaurants, such as those at the Hotel Savoy (p70), Helvetia & Bristol (p70), Gallery Hotel Art (p71) and JK Place (p71).

Florence al Fresco

In the dog days of summer you will want to eat well and under the stars. Among the most tempting candidates are Enoteca Fuoriporta (p58), Trattoria dei 13 Gobbi (p55), Osteria Santo Spirito (p59) and La Terrazza del Principe (p59).

Cena a Due

For a romantic evening for two, book you and yours into Trattoria Cavolo Nero (p60), Oliviero (p53) or, for a special occasion, Enoteca Pinchiorri (p56).

No More Pasta!!!

When you can't face another plate of pasta, head to Momoyama (p59), Ruth's (p57) or Ristorante Cibrèo (p57).

---

pesky pigeons gather to wolf down cheap and tasty Tuscan staples such as tripe, pasta and *pappa al pomodoro*.
☎ 055 21 99 49 ✉ Mercato Centrale 🕒 7am-2pm Mon-Sat 🚌 1, 6, 7, 10, 11 & 17 ♿

Il Vegetariano (3, E3)

Vegetarian €

A bit of a trek from the centre (about 1km northeast of the station) but well worth the leather if you're tired of the same old, same old. This informal restaurant with communal tables has a wonderful salad bar – with market-fresh ingredients. There's a pleasant outdoor area in which to savour an ever-changing cavalcade of global vegetarian specialities.

☎ 055 47 50 30 ✉ Via delle Ruote 30/r 🕒 lunch & dinner Tue-Fri, dinner only Sat & Sun 🚌 4, 12 & 20 ♿ V

Trattoria Mario (3, D4)

Tuscan €

Avoid the queues and arrive early at this wonderfully homely family-run trattoria, an excellent place to sink

your teeth into the famous *bistecca fiorentina* or any number of Tuscan classics. They only serve lunch and were long assailed almost exclusively by famished market workers. No credit cards.

☎ 055 21 85 50 ✉ Via Rosina 2/r 🕒 lunch only Mon-Sat 🚌 1, 6, 7, 10, 11 & 17 ♿ V

SANTA MARIA NOVELLA

Da il Latini (4, B4)

Tuscan €€

If you're in a group – or are feeling particularly sociable – this cavernous place is perfect for a rousing night of passable house wine and humongous portions of hearty, predominantly meaty fare beneath more dead pigs than you could shake a fork at. Come early, bring freezer bags and be prepared to queue as they don't take reservations.

☎ 055 21 09 16 ✉ Via dei Palchetti 🕒 lunch & dinner 🚌 6 & A ♿

I Quattro Amici (3, B4)

Seafood €€€

In a handy position just around the corner from the railway station, you can

Lunch at the popular Trattoria Mario is worth the wait

No need to ham it up at Da il Latini (opposite)

start eating well as soon as you get of the train. One of a handful of eateries in Florence that is serious about its fish, the 'Four Friends' is as friendly as it sounds and there's not a steak in sight. ☎ 055 21 54 13 ⊠ Via degli Orti Oricellari 29 🕑 lunch & dinner 🚍 26, 27, 35 & D ♿

Osteria dei Cento Poveri
(3, C5)
Modern Italian €€€
These days the 'hostel of a hundred poor people' focuses almost exclusively on cashed-up tourists who enjoy contemporary twists on Tuscan classics – as well as some from Puglia and a daily fish special – in this tiny and congenial place in a not so congenial part of town. ☎ 055 21 88 46 ⊠ Via Palazzuolo 31/r 🕑 dinner only Tue-Sat, lunch & dinner Sun 🚍 11, 36, 37 & A ♿

Trattoria Coco Lezzone
(4, B5)
Modern Tuscan €€€
A significant contributor to Luciano Pavarotti's ample

girth, 'the big, fat cook' is an old-fashioned trattoria with a big reputation, hefty prices, gargantuan portions of top-notch Tuscan grub and, unbelievably, no coffee! ☎ 055 28 71 78 ⊠ Via Parioncino 26/r 🕑 lunch & dinner Mon-Sat 🚍 A

Trattoria dei 13 Gobbi
(3, B5)
Modern Tuscan €€
For rustic comforts, sophisticated food, agreeable service and the company of locals, you'll be hard pressed to top this welcoming spot. There's a lovely plant-filled inner courtyard and the kitchen is more relaxed about closing time than most other places should you have spent lunch seeing the sights. ☎ 055 28 40 15 ⊠ Via del Porcellana 9/r 🕑 lunch & dinner Tue-Sat 🚍 A ♿ V

SANTA CROCE

Antico Noè (7, B3)
Sandwich Bar €
It isn't pretty in this arcade but if you want to choose from almost 20 delicious,

heaped and filling take-away sandwiches from this Florentine institution, you'll have to run the gauntlet of the hobos. There's also reasonable food at the comfy café next door. ☎ 055 234 08 38 ⊠ Volta di San Piero 6/r 🕑 noon-midnight Mon-Sat 🚍 14 & 23 V

Boccadama (7, A5)
Enoteca €€
Mobbed by tourists during the day, this place and its location are best appreciated in the evenings when the locals reclaim them. There's a small menu of light and original dishes to complement the standard *enoteca* fare. The young staff are warm and friendly, and you can choose from hundreds of wine labels. ☎ 055 24 36 40 🖵 www .boccadama.it ⊠ Piazza di Santa Croce 25-26/r 🕑 lunch & dinner Mon-Sat 🚍 C V

Danny Rock (7, A4)
Italian €
All right, the name doesn't sound promising but this

A LOAD OF TRIPE

When you come across a hot-dog stand in Florence, bear in mind that there are no hot-dog stands in Florence. Instead, you can get the very Florentine fast-food *lampredotto* (boiled tripe in a bun dripping with hot chilli sauce). For €2 to €3, you also get a cup of rough wine. *Trippai* (tripe stands) are scattered about the city and tend to finish up about 3pm. An excellent example of the species is **La Tripperia da Sergio e Pier Paolo** (7, C4; Via de' Macci; ☺ 8.30am-7pm Mon-Sat Sep-May, 8.30am-3pm Mon-Sat Jun & Jul; bus C).

bright and metallic US-style hang-out pulsates with young locals and foreigners most nights, and has a huge international menu incorporating better-than-expected crepes, huge salads, pizzas and burgers.
☎ 055 234 03 07 🖳 www .dannyrock.it ✉ Via de' Pandolfini ☺ 7pm-3am 🚍 A ♿ Ⓥ

Enoteca Pinchiorri (7, B4)
Modern Tuscan €€€€
Hallowed turf in Italian gastronomy, this Michelin-starred place occupies an elegant *palazzo* with a delightful inner courtyard. It's

famous for its tiddly portions of astounding contemporary Tuscan fare and a cellar chock-a-block with 80,000 wines. Trust the tasting menus – Tuscan, seasonal and vegetarian – and the suave sommeliers.
☎ 055 24 27 77 🖳 www .enotecapinchiorri.com ✉ Via Ghibellina 87 ☺ lunch-dinner Tue-Sat 🚍 14 ♿ Ⓥ

Finisterrae (7, B4)
Fusion €€
With its labyrinth of interlocking dining halls and Arabesque lounges, this place screams (softly) 'chill!' as

you wander in. Mood music combines with candlelight to create the kind of setting you might imagine in certain restaurants in, well, Soho. Foodwise, you're looking at simple Italian or Maghreb fare. Pop by for a Sunday brunch.
☎ 055 24 19 32 ✉ Via de' Pepi 3-5/r ☺ lunch & dinner Wed-Sun, dinner only Mon & Tue 🚍 C

Gelateria Vivoli (7, A4)
Gelateria €
The unrelenting peer pressure to try the *gelati* here, considered by many to be the best in Florence, is almost enough to put you off. It's relatively expensive, cups are teeny weeny, and the atmosphere is solemn, but all's forgiven when you taste the *gelati,* the flavours of which will be etched on your palate long after you've returned home.
☎ 055 29 23 34 ✉ Via Isola delle Stinche 7/r ☺ 9am-1am Tue-Sun 🚍 A ♿ Ⓥ

Il Pizzaiuolo (7, C4)
Pizzeria €€
It's the best place in town for the famous Neapolitan pizzas (thin base with light puffy edges), staff and many ingredients here hail from Naples and there are almost 30 different toppings. Pull up to small wooden tables perfect for solo diners and small groups and join the throngs of expectant locals staring at the glow from the traditional wood-fired oven.
☎ 055 24 11 71 ✉ Via de' Macci 113/r ☺ lunch & dinner Mon-Sat 🚍 C ♿ Ⓥ

NOTHING TO WINE ABOUT

Tuscany is awash with the nectar of the vine. The bulk of its better known drops are reds made with the local Sangiovese grape. Il Chianti, an area roughly between Florence and Siena, produces much of the wine, from simple table plonk to the fine wines grouped together as **Chianti Classico**, **Brunello di Montalcino**, and **Vino Nobile di Montepulciano**, from the villages of Montalcino and Montepulciano in the south of Tuscany, are among the region's most prized reds.

Less known are some outstanding whites, including **Vernaccia di San Gimignano** (steely, aromatic and fruity). **Vin Santo** ('holy wine') is Tuscany's splendid dessert wine, made from semi-dried Trebbiano Toscano grapes.

The so-called Super Tuscans lie outside the complicated Italian DOC and DOCG wine classification systems. They may not respect the rules, but count among some of the most exciting wines being produced in Tuscany today largely because of their feisty iconoclasm.

Osteria de' Benci (3, A5)
Italian €€
Perennially popular with blow-ins and locals who seem to gather here in groups, the mainly Tuscan food is seasonal – light in summer, heartier in winter – but always on the mark. Street level and outside are cosier than the crammed brick-vaulted cellar where you'll end up if you don't book.
☎ 055 234 49 23 ⊠ Via de' Benci 13/r ⏱ lunch & dinner Mon-Sat 🚌 13, 23, B & C Ⓥ

Ristorante Cibrèo (7, C4)
Modern Tuscan €€€€
Famous for being famous – as you will see from the number of guidebook-clutching tourists – Cibrèo offers an elegantly simple dining atmosphere for recherché Tuscan cooking in which pasta has no place. The same people run a couple of other eateries and café on the same street.
☎ 055 234 11 00 ⊠ Via de' Macci 118/r ⏱ lunch & dinner Tue-Sat Sep-Jul 🚌 C Ⓥ

Ruth's (7, C3)
Middle Eastern €
As long as you avoid the house wine, the clean and simple flavours of this kosher vegetarian and fish restaurant next to the synagogue make for a pleasant change from Tuscan tucker. Ruth's dish is a plateful of titbits including couscous, hummus and falafel.
☎ 055 248 08 88 ⊠ Via Luigi Carlo Farini 2/a ⏱ lunch & dinner Sun-Thu, lunch only Fri 🚌 C ♿ Ⓥ

Samovar (7, D3)
Russian Fusion €€€
Head through the heavy red drapes into this intriguing Med-Russian-fusion den, a low-lit Buddha Bar from the steppes, where you might opt for a steaming stroganoff or sashimi on a skewer. There's no culinary reverence in this deliberately iconoclastic big-city style chilled dining locale.
☎ 055 24 49 35 ⊠ Via della Mattonaia 51/r ⏱ dinner only Mon-Sat 🚌 6, 31 & 32

Sésame (7, C5)
Med-Moroccan Fusion €€€
The kind of place you could wear sunglasses at night, just to feel as mysterious as the food combos. You can opt for Moroccan dishes or a pricey inventive Mediterranean menu.
☎ 055 200 18 31 ⊠ Via delle Conce 20/r ⏱ dinner only Tue-Sun 🚌 C Ⓥ

OLTRARNO

All'Antico Ristoro di Cambi (3, A6)
Tuscan €€
Run by the Cambi family since the 1940s – and barely

Try out new wines at Le Volpi e l'Uva (p59)

changed since. All'Antico Ristoro di Cambi is a bustling and endearing trattoria reliable for *bistecca alla fiorentina,* traditional Tuscan soups and seasonal salads, although they could do with a cushion or two on the hard wooden chairs.
☎ 055 21 71 34 ☒ Via Sant'Onofrio 1 🕙 lunch & dinner Mon-Sat 🚌 6 & D 🚲 Ⓥ

Al Tranvai (3, A7)
Tuscan €€
Not just another simple and atmospheric trattoria – okay, maybe it is – this place has a penchant for *trippa alla fiorentina* (tripe) and other grisly bits as well as the usual Tuscan fare. The combination is so popular with the locals that tables usually end up being shared.
☎ 055 22 51 97 ☒ Piazza Torquato Tasso 14/r 🕙 7.30-10.30pm Mon-Fri 🚌 12, 13 & D 🚲

Borgo San Jacopo (4, C7)
Modern Italian €€€€
The designer folks behind Ferragamo's Hotel Lungarno have brought similar flare to this hip riverside design restaurant. Try for a low-lit table by the window and watch the sun set on the Arno as you indulge in modern, inventive dishes.
☎ 055 28 16 61 ☒ Borgo San Jacopo 62/r 🕙 dinner only Wed-Mon 🚌 D Ⓥ

Enoteca Fuoriporta (3, E8)
Enoteca €€
After sunset at Piazzale Michelangelo, flop down the hill to this convivial *enoteca* in the shadow of the old city gate. Join the local clamour in the bar or set yourself on the pleasant outdoor terrace and explore the tasty menu (try the *burata,* a delicious clump of mozzarella from Puglia) and wash down with a series of wines by the glass.

☎ 055 234 24 83 🖳 www .fuoriporta.it ☒ Via Monte alle Croci 🕙 lunch & dinner Mon-Sat 🚌 13, 23 & D 🚲 Ⓥ

Fuor d'Acqua (3, A6)
Seafood €€
One of only a handful of good seafood and fish restaurants in this largely meat-eating town, 'Out of Water' proposes a menu of sea critters that changes in line with what the fisherfolk have been able to catch off the Tuscan coast. The kitchen closes at 11.30pm, late by Florentine standards!
☎ 055 22 22 99 ☒ Via Pisana 37/r 🕙 dinner only Mon-Sat 🚌 6 🚲

Il Santo Bevitore (3, B6)
Tuscan €€
Young staff dash about beneath the vaults of this popular and serious eatery. The dark timber tables are the perfect support for a

Chefs at Ristorante Beccofino (opposite) give an innovative touch to Tuscan fare

bottle of deep Tuscan red. Then you'll need to choose some grub from the limited Tuscan menu, replete with classic dishes.

☎ 055 21 12 64 ✉ Via dello Spirito Santo 64-66/r ☺ lunch & dinner Tue-Sun 🚌 6 & D ♿

Il Vico del Carmine
(3, A6)
Pizzeria €€
Away from the madding crowds of central Florence they have created a little piece of Naples – quite literally a lane typical of the southern city. This makes the ideal setting for good Neapolitan pizza, and the ingredients for all their dishes are said to come from the Campania region around Naples.

☎ 055 233 68 62 ✉ Via Pisana 40/r ☺ lunch & dinner Tue-Sun 🚌 6 ♿

La Terrazza del Principe
(1, E3)
Modern Tuscan €€€€
Leave Florence without leaving Florence. From your garden table breathe in the bucolic views looking back to the south side of the city, mostly blocked from view by the greenery. The culinary theme is inventive Tuscan.

☎ 055 22 41 04 ✉ Viale Machiavelli 10 ☺ lunch & dinner 🚌 12 & 13

Le Volpi e l'Uva (4, C7)
Snacks €
'The Foxes and the Grape' is hidden away off the Oltrarno end of the Ponte Vecchio. Sample the cheese treasures, have a gourmet *tramezzino* (sandwich triangle) and try out new wines.

The atmospheric Trattoria Cavolo Nero (p60)

☎ 055 239 81 32 ✉ Piazza de' Rossi 1/r ☺ 11am-8pm Mon-Sat 🚌 D ♿

Momoyama (3, B6)
Japanese €€€
Ambrosia for the jaded palate, this stylish and cosy place is one of the best restaurants in town and a magnet for well-heeled trendies. It specialises in exquisitely presented Japanese and 'inventive cuisine' – stick to the Japanese and you won't be disappointed.

☎ 055 29 18 40 ✉ Borgo San Frediano 10/r ☺ dinner only Tue-Sun 🚌 6 & D

Osteria Santo Spirito
(3, B7)
Italian €€
The crayoned, tatty menu at this popular place – outside which expectant diners and smoking kitchen staff mingle before it opens (not a second before time) – encompasses the best of Italian fare, prepared simply and delivered in huge portions on fabulous oversized, hand-painted plates.

☎ 055 238 23 83 ✉ Piazza Santo Spirito 16/r ☺ lunch & dinner 🚌 D ♿ Ⓥ

Ristorante Beccofino
(4, A6)
Modern Italian €€€€
The foreign legion of chefs and management at this sleek restaurant keep their standards high with their innovative Tuscan fare, and Beccofino is a hot spot for young Florentines. Staff are smooth and courteous, the soundtrack is groovy and there's a superb list of wines.

☎ 055 29 00 76 ✉ Piazza degli Scarlatti 1/r ☺ lunch & dinner Tue-Sun 🚌 6

Trattoria Casalinga
(4, A8)
Traditional Tuscan €
On a small street leading to Piazza Santo Spirito, this bright and bustling trattoria is a local favourite and manages to keep its traditions

intact despite the tourist madness going on around it.
☎ 055 21 86 24 ✉ Via de' Michelozzi 9/r ☻ lunch & dinner Mon-Sat 🚌 11, 36 & 37

Trattoria Cavolo Nero
(3, B7)
Mediterranean €€€
Well off the main tourist trails – but the 'secret' of most concierges – the Tuscan 'black cabbage' is an elegant and intimate restaurant with flattering lighting and a menu that favours meat-eaters but offers some tempting soups too. Keep room for dessert.
☎ 055 29 47 44 ✉ Via dell'Ardiglione 22 ☻ lunch & dinner Tue-Sat 🚌 11, 36 & 37

Trattoria Napoleone
(3, B6)
Tuscan & Pizzeria €€
Carnivores will no doubt want to call by here for an aptly named *filetto alla Napoleone,* a handsome steak dressed in a vinegar and mustard sauce. The pizzas are also reasonable. A down side is that the outdoor dining area on those hot summer nights is in the middle of a car park. An upside is that you can order one in until 12.30am!
☎ 055 28 10 15 ✉ Piazza del Carmine 24 ☻ dinner only 🚌 D

COFFEE CULTURE & TERRIBLE TEA

For many Italians a good coffee is essential to survival. It is only natural then, as Eskimos with snow and ice, that they should have myriad types and terms. Milky coffee, either caffè latte or the frothy cappuccino version, is a morning drink only. **Espresso** (a short, strong shot of coffee) is the most popular cup. A **doppio espresso** is a double shot and may catapult you through the window. A **caffè macchiato** is an espresso with a dash of frothy milk, while a **latte macchiato** is a hot milk with a dash of coffee. A **caffè lungo/doppio/americano** is a long, watered-down espresso. A **corretto** is an espresso 'corrected' with a dash of grappa or other strong alcohol.

Tea barely rates a mention and is often served as a cup of lukewarm water with teabag. Requests for milk will be carried out but met with incredulity.

Florence boasts some fine historic cafés, especially on Piazza della Repubblica. If you can painlessly part with €3.50 for a coffee or €5.50 for a hot chocolate at a terrace table, do some people watching at these century-old (or older) establishments:

- **Café Concerto Paszkowski** (4, D4; ☎ 055 21 02 36; Piazza della Repubblica 31-35/r; ☻ 7am-2am Tue-Sun; bus A)
- **Gilli** (4, D4; ☎ 055 21 38 96; Piazza della Repubblica 39/r; coffee on the square €3.50; ☻ 8am-1am Wed-Sun; bus A)
- **Giubbe Rosse** (4, D4; ☎ 055 21 22 80; Piazza della Repubblica 13-14/r; ☻ 8am-2am; bus A)
- **Rivoire** (4, D5; ☎ 055 21 44 12; Piazza della Signoria 4/r; ☻ 8am-11pm Tue-Sun; bus B)

Entertainment

It's only at night you realise that Florence is a provincial town. However, while it's not exactly *hopping*, there is plenty to keep you engaged for at least a few days.

Young foreign students and the silver-tongued – and frequently silver-haired – local men who pursue them largely fuel the mainstream nightlife. Many bars in the centre are the preserve of foreign blow-ins, just as some, usually a little further out, are clearly favoured by locals. Florentines can make or break a business. Guided by a fickle herd instinct, the whole city seems to collectively judge which places are in and which are out. Last year's winner is this year's loser. In summer especially, many Florentines elect the various open-air events (see the Summer Frolics boxed text, p68), a small selection of hip bars (often with terrace), or to escape the city altogether.

A handful of clubs, from mainstream pop to a couple of hedonistic gay venues, keep people happy dancing and prancing in the wee hours.

If theatre, dance, opera or classical music are more your thing, you'll be well catered for with several excellent venues regularly hosting local and international events.

Consult the monthly listings magazine *Firenze Spettacolo* (€1.60), which has a small English section and is available at newsstands. Also look out for the some of the free gigs publications around certain bars. They include *Zero* and *Nightfly*.

Get your theatre tickets from **Box Office** (3, B4; ☎ 055 21 08 04; www .boxol.it; Via Luigi Alamanni 39; ☺ 3.30-7.30pm Mon, 10am-7pm Tue-Sat).

WAVING THE FLAG

Wherever there's a festival in Florence and Tuscany, you're likely to see extravagant displays of medieval pageantry and *sbandieratori* (flag throwers) doing their thing. The ancient practice of flag throwing evokes the pride with which soldiers used to protect their colours, and celebrates the skills of the flag bearers, who used their banners to send signals to the troops. They probably didn't juggle their flags, toss them high in the air and hope to catch them before the poles impaled onlooking tourists, as they do in various Tuscan piazzas today, but it's a splendid spectacle all the same.

Pageantry and *sbandieratori* (flag-throwers) in front of the Duomo

SPECIAL EVENTS

January
New Year (1 January) Outdoor events, including a parade of boats on the Arno.
Epiphany (6 January) Parade of the *Re Magi* (Three Wise Men).

February
Carnevale (10 days leading up to Shrove Tuesday) A low-key affair of confetti scattering and children in fancy dress.

March
Festa della Donna (International Women's Day; 8 March) Women are given sprigs of yellow mimosa and hit the town.

April
Scoppio del Carro (Explosion of the Cart; Easter Sunday) A 15th-century ritual where an ox-drawn cart laden with fireworks is led to the Duomo by flag throwers and musicians, and the fireworks are set off by a rocket on a wire.

May
Festa del Grillo (The Cricket Festival; Ascension Day) A welcome to spring in which Florentine families traditionally packed off for picnics at Le Cascine and dads hunted for crickets for their kids, or bought them ready trapped. Until 2001, that is, when the town hall ordered only models be used in the interests of insect welfare. Tradition says men also placed crickets at the door of their lovers.

June
Festa di San Giovanni (Feast of St John; 24 June) Celebrations, fireworks and flag throwers.
Gioco del Calcio Storico (Historical Football Game; played over several Sundays in June) Four teams of bare-chested gents representing historic town districts fight for the prize (a calf) in this few-rules medieval version of football held in Piazza di Santa Croce.

September
Festa della Rificolona (Paper Lantern Festival; 1st Sunday of September) Processions of children with paper lanterns celebrate the eve of Our Lady's supposed birthday on 7 September.

October
Musica dei Popoli (World Music Festival; throughout October and November) Held at Auditorium Flog (see p66).

November
Firenze Marathon (Held towards the end of the month) The high-speed walking tour of Florence.

BARS

Santa Croce and the Oltrarno are – in our opinion – among the best areas in Florence for fun after dark, although there are also a few smart establishments peppered throughout the city's centre. While thirsty foreigners often zero in on UK-style pubs with very generous happy hours, most locals pursue the latest trendy bars putting on an *aperitivo*, involving cocktails and often generous, imaginative bar snacks. Many bars close for the hot Florentine summer.

Cabiria (4, A7)
Bustling day and night, this funky little music bar attracts a largely local and chilled-out crew, drawn by consistently good tunes and a buzz that spills out onto Piazza Santo Spirito in summer.
☎ 055 21 57 32 ✉ Piazza Santo Spirito 4/r ⏰ 11am-1.30am Wed-Mon 🚌 D

Caffè La Torre (7, C6)
The colour red is the dominant theme, and the late, late closing time has locals hovering in and around this drinkers' honey pot like so many very thirsty bees. Caffè La Torre in fact is a rather cool location, with a mostly chilled mix of music, which only helps to maintain its popularity at all hours.
☎ 055 68 06 43 ✉ Lungarno Benvenuto Cellini 65/r ⏰ 8.30am-4am 🚌 12, 13, 23 & D

Capocaccia (4, B5)

Molto trendy, Capocaccia is an elegant café-bar with an alternative menu of snacks by day and is one of *the* places to be seen at night, when cool Florentines snuggle up to other cool Florentines and the self-conscious bonhomie spills out onto the street. Throw in the occasional DJ and you'll understand why it's almost impossible to get your *motorino* through the throng.
☎ 055 21 07 51 ⊠ Lungarno Corsini 12-14/r ☽ noon-4pm Mon, noon-1am Tue-Sun ☐ B

Cocktails at Capocaccia is a must

Il Rifrullo (3, E8)

A great bar on a quiet corner of San Niccolò, this place gets a chirpy, suave crowd and is a wonderful spot to mingle with the locals, refuel on an impressive spread of *aperitivi* and slip into delicious cocktails. Hunker down inside, sit down on the pavement terrace or opt for a shady spot on the back terrace.
☎ 055 234 26 21 ⊠ Via di San Niccolò 55/r ☽ 9am-1am ☐ 12, 13, 23 & D

Joshua Tree (3, B5)

Scruffy and relaxed, this is a tavern where bullshit is barred and the only Irish 'themes' come by way of Murphy's stout, moody shades of green and conviviality by the keg. It gets a lot louder as the night goes on but then don't we all?
⊠ Via della Scala 41 ☽ 4pm-1am ☐ 11, 36, 37 & A

Kikuya Pub (7, A5)

Larger than usual cocktails – although it's really not that kind of place – and a predominantly foreign crowd are found in this traditional-looking English bar, where there's occasional live music and a good selection of English beer. Local boys visit in twos to check on the number of foreign girls drinking here (and to see what state they're in).
☎ 055 234 48 79 ⊠ Via de' Benci 43/r ☽ 7pm-3am ☐ B & C

La Dolce Vita (3, B7)

One of the most popular pre-club hang-outs, this place gets so packed with wealthy wannabes that you might never see the bar. An outdoor terrace helps you forget you're in a car park, although the regulars don't quite make you feel like you're at home.
☎ 055 28 45 95 ⊠ Piazza del Carmine 6/r ☽ 8pm-1am Mon-Thu, 8pm-3am Fri-Sun ☐ D

Mamma (3, A6)

On those warm summer nights half of Florence seems to be here (the other half is probably on holiday). Tables on the grass in the shadow of the illuminated city walls, a series of bars and even some Bedouin-style tent space attract hordes of tanned and showy locals.
☎ 055 233 67 76 ⊠ Lungarno di Santa Rosa ☽ 7pm-2am Mon-Thu, 7pm-3am Fri & Sat ☐ 6 & D

Montecarla (4, F9)

Leopard skins, gaudy cushions, plush drapes, plastic flowers and moody corners abound if you don't mind the membership here. They say it was never a bordello but we're not convinced.
☎ 055 234 02 59 ⊠ Via de' Bardi 2 ☽ 8pm-4am Thu-Tue ☐ 13, 23 & D

Negroni (7, A6)

One of the city's hippest bars for sipping, well, a Negroni (a Campari and gin–based cocktail) and tucking into the Milan-style bar buffet at the generously long *aperitivo* hour. A DJ spins some not-too-intense club sounds out the back.

Subtle it's not, but the Rex Caffè is one of the best

☎ 055 24 36 47 ✉ Via dei Renai 17/r ⏲ 8am-2am Mon-Sat, 6pm-2am Sun 🚌 12, 13, 23 & D

Rex Caffè (7, B3)

Smooth cocktails, big beats, coquettish staff and a cosy back room (perhaps in that order) combine to make this one of the best bars in Florence. The Gaudì-esque interior is an elegant, colourful mess, but the vibe is convivial and the tunes are guaranteed to make your bum wiggle.

☎ 055 248 03 31 ✉ Via Fiesolana 25/r ⏲ 5pm-3am Sep-May 🚌 C

Salamanca (7, B4)

This pseudo-Spanish joint has an attractive horseshoe bar but you won't get near it at weekends when the place reverberates to flamenco rock and fills to the rafters with foreign girls and local boys. Dress to sweat and don't underestimate the cocktails.

☎ 055 234 54 52 ✉ Via Ghibellina 80/r ⏲ 7pm-2am 🚌 14

Sant'Ambrogio Caffè (7, C4)

A truly local bar, this place draws a congenial crew of smart 30-somethings and funkier arty types. Tables are set up outside in summer, and there are reasonable snacks during the day.

☎ 055 24 10 35 ✉ Piazza Sant'Ambrogio 7/r ⏲ 9am-2am Mon-Sat 🚌 C

Slowly (4, C5)

A busy spot that attracts frizzy-haired ladies with euro-trash wardrobes and slick Don Giovannis checking out the talent from behind designer shades. Cocktails are colourful and generous and the snacks quite edible.

☎ 055 264 53 54 ✉ Via Porta Rossa 63/r ⏲ noon-2.30am Mon-Sat, 6pm-2.30am Sun 🚌 A

William (7, A5)

Although it's another of the English-style contingent (of which you may have noticed there is no shortage), this cavernous drinking den tends to attract groups of young Florentines in search of a pint of ale rather than gangs of holiday-makers in search of six.

☎ 055 246 98 00 ✉ Via Magliabechi 7/r ⏲ 6pm-2am 🚌 C

Zoe (7, A6)

Long-haired boys and short-skirted girls flock to sassy and sexy Zoe's neon red sign, behind which you can enjoy meaty acid jazz while sitting on long, black-leather couches against ruby-red walls and savouring the eye candy. ☎ 055 24 31 11 ✉ Via dei Renai 13/r ☼ 3pm-2am Apr-Oct, 6pm-2am Tue-Sun Nov-Mar ☒ 12, 13, 23 & D

DANCE CLUBS

Many Florentine clubs aim for the lowest common denominator and, if you're into serious clubbing, they may feel more like school discos and the music blasts from the past. Some clubs don't even have DJs, relying instead on compilation CDs. We've listed a selection of the better ones. In some spots foreign students with ID are allowed in free.

Central Park (1, D2)
Catering for a broad local and international crew, this party in the park has four dance zones with sounds ranging from top vocal house to awful Italian pop. The outdoor dance area is a summer must. ☎ 055 35 35 05 ✉ Via Fosso Macinante 2, Parco delle Cascine € €20

> **YOUR PAYING CARD**
> Some venues operate an annoying card system, whereby you saunter in for free but must pay to get out. You'll be given a small card to get stamped every time you buy a drink, and then you pay your bill on the way out. You pay a minimum amount whether you've drunk anything or not.

☼ 11pm-6am Tue-Sat ☒ 1, 9, 12, 13, 16, 26, 27, 80 & B

Exmud (7, A5)
This (literally) underground club serves up a staple of house anthems to a regular and lively young posse. There's a cocktail lounge and a chilled-out courtyard. ☎ 055 263 85 83 ☐ www .exmud.it ✉ Corso dei Tintori 4 € €10-15 ☼ 9pm-4am Mon, Thu-Sat ☒ B & C

Meccanò (1, D2)
Of the three sprawling dance spaces the main one is largely given over to a rhythmic crew of go-go dancers. Thursday is house night at Meccanò but really any day is quite all right too. And you may well find a good sprinkling of locals in here alongside the

inevitable foreign student brigade. ☎ 055 33 13 71 ✉ Viale degli Olmi 1 € €20 ☼ 11pm-5am Tue-Sat ☒ 1, 9, 12, 13, 16, 26, 27, 80 & B

Universale (1, D2)
There's something for almost everyone here. Housed in the shell of an old theatre, this 'lifestyle club' incorporates restaurant, bar and club areas, and is not as dodgy as it sounds. The occasional live music is bigger and better than the Florentine norm but it's the solid staple of local, national and even international DJs that keeps people coming back. ☎ 055 22 11 22 ✉ Via Pisana 77/r € €10-15 (incl first drink) ☼ 8pm-3am Wed-Sun Sep-May ☒ 6

Yab (4, C5)
Older clubbers readily flock to this central favourite where there's a good mix of top-drawer sounds throughout the week and with on-the-minute hip-hop Mondays. A huge dance floor is flanked with raised bars which are perfect for wiggling and watching – and watching and wiggling. ☎ 055 21 51 60 ✉ Via de' Sassetti 5/r € up to €20 ☼ Mon-Sat Oct–late May, Mon only Jun-Sep ☒ 6 & A

Vinyl still has its place...

LIVE MUSIC

Florence certainly ain't at the cutting edge in the live-music stakes; most central venues offer the same standard fare of cover bands which means you'll have to go out into the suburbs to hear original local and touring bands. Occasionally a big act swings through town, accommodated at Tenax or the football stadium (p68).

Auditorium Flog (1, E2)
Regular live gigs from genre-spanning local and touring bands are the go at this big venue, usually followed by DJs spinning anything from old-school house to electronica. If you're here in October/November and like your world music, make sure to catch the terrific Musica dei Popoli festival.
☎ 055 49 04 37 ☐ www .flog.it ✉ Via M Mercati 24/b € free–€10 ☽ 10pm–4am ☒ 4, 8, 14, 20 & 28

Bebop (7, A2)
There's no rhyme – sometimes not even reason – to the music played here, although you might find something to suit on its menu of jazz, blues and country. Admission is usually free and the atmosphere laid-back.
☎ 055 239 65 44 ✉ Via dei Servi 76/r € free–€10 ☽ 8pm–2am Mon-Sat ☒ C

Jazz Club (7, B3)
Refreshingly uncool, this is the best place to hear live jazz on Friday and Saturday nights as well as jamming sessions on Tuesday and maybe blues and Latin fillers at other times.
☎ 055 247 97 00 ✉ Via Nuova de' Caccini 3 € membership €6 ☽ 9.30pm-1am Sun-Thu, 9.30pm-2am Fri & Sat ☒ C

Tenax (1, C1)
This is where the big names play when they come to town and it's also a good place to check the pulse of the Italian scene. When the

bands clear, the best local DJs take over and the massive raised dance floor pumps to progressive house, big beat and hip-hop.
☎ 055 30 81 60 ☐ www .tenax.org ✉ Via Pratese 46 € free–€20 ☽ 10pm-4am Tue-Sun ☒ 29 & 30

GAY & LESBIAN FLORENCE

Florence has a healthy gay scene for a city of its size when it's compared to the rest of Italy. Choose from several dedicated venues which includes Italy's first gay discotheque – as well as a small group of welcoming mixed bars. Several straight clubs also put on popular gay nights. The city's gay venuees are mainly around Santa Croce.

Crisco (7, A3)
Gyrating choons and cruising are the norm at this leather 'n' Levis men-only bar, which is particularly popular with

The Jazz Club – don't miss it!

Y.A.G Bar sign on Via de'Macci

the hirsute. There are x-rated videos and dark rooms.

☎ 055 248 05 80 ⊠ Via Sant'Egidio 43/r ⏲ 8pm-4am Sun & Mon & Wed & Thu, 8pm-6am Fri & Sat 🚌 14 & 23

Piccolo Café (7, A5)
Relaxed and unruffled, this bar has a cool metallic ceiling adorned with phallic light bulbs, and attracts a mixed crowd of gays and lesbians.

☎ 055 200 10 57 ⊠ Borgo Santa Croce 23/r ⏲ 5pm-2am 🚌 C

Tabasco (4, D5)
Only boys get the nod at Italy's oldest gay disco, the perfect place if you're feeling frisky. There's a disco, cocktail bar and dark room in *the* most central location, just off Piazza della Signoria. Dress code is as loose as the behaviour.

☎ 055 21 30 00 💻 www .tabascogay.it ⊠ Piazza di Santa Cecilia 3/r ⏲ 8pm-4am, disco until 6am Tue, Fri & Sat 🚌 A

Y.A.G Bar (7, C5)
There's a warm and fuzzy atmosphere at this spacious dance bar, invariably full of cute young guys and a sprinkling of lesbians. It gets packed by midnight.

☎ 055 246 90 22 ⊠ Via de' Macci 8/r ⏲ 7pm-3am 🚌 C

CINEMAS

While dubbing of foreign-language films is prevalent, several venues show films in the *versione originale* (original language). This means films in English with Italian subtitles. At most cinemas there are three or four sessions daily, the latest starting between 10pm and 10.45pm. Wednesday is cheap cinema day, when tickets cost €5. Normally they cost around €7.20.

Cinema Fulgor (3, B5)
Thursday night is mainstream English-language movie night here, and you can get

discount passes for groups or multiple sessions.

☎ 055 238 18 81 ⊠ Via Maso Finiguerra 22/r ⏲ Sep-Jul 🚌 B

Odeon Cinehall (4, C4)
This is the main location for seeing flicks in their original language with subtitles, screened on Mondays and Tuesdays.

☎ 055 21 40 68 💻 www .cinehall.it ⊠ Piazza degli Strozzi 1 ⏲ Oct-Jun 🚌 6 & A

THEATRE, DANCE, CLASSICAL MUSIC & OPERA

To find out what's on where, you should check out *Firenze Spettacolo*. We've listed some of the many venues which stage events from across the wide range of arts.

Teatro Comunale (3, A5)
Concerts, opera and dance are the staples at this old but utilitarian 2000-seater. You can catch all three of these arts in May and June each year when the theatre hosts the two-month Maggio Musicale Fiorentina festival. MaggioDanza is the resident dance company and puts on regular ballet performances and hosts visiting shows.

☎ 800 11 22 11 💻 www .maggiofiorentino.com ⊠ Corso Italia 12 € varies 🚌 B

Teatro della Limonaia (1, D1)
Fringe theatre on the fringe of Florence, this small but

atmospheric theatre also hosts the Intercity Festival in late summer, when contemporary theatre companies from different international capitals are invited to stage their performances – which can include dance and theatre – here.

☎ 055 44 08 52 🖳 www .teatrodellalimonaia.it ✉ Via Gramsci 426, Sesto Fiorentino € €8-12 🚌 2 & 28A

Teatro della Pergola (7, A3)

Italy's oldest theatre is a cosy place in which to hear chamber music from international companies, organised by the Amici della Musica. It also hosts occasional ballet, opera and drama.

☎ 055 247 96 51 🖳 www .pergola.firenze.it ✉ Via della Pergola 18 € varies 🚌 C

Teatro Verdi (7, A4)

There are seasons of drama, opera, concerts and dance in this 19th-century theatre – built on the site of a 14th-century prison – but it's best known as the place to hear the 40-strong Orchestra Regionale Toscana (ORT).

☎ 055 21 23 20 🖳 www .teatroverdifirenze.it ✉ Via Ghibellina 99 € up to €15 for classical concerts ⏲ Oct-Apr 🚌 14 & A

SPORT

Football

Come to the 45,000-seater **Stadio Comunale 'Artemio Franchi'** (1, F2; ☎ 055 50 32 61; www.acffiorentina.it; Viale Manfredo Fanti 4, Campo di Marte) and watch the miraculous Violas. After the humiliation of bankruptcy and relegation beyond the outer galaxy, they managed to leapfrog divisions back into Serie A in 2004, where they have since hung on by the skin of their teeth. Home games usually take place every second Sunday at 3pm. For tickets contact Box Office (see p61) or just walk up before kick-off.

Motorsport

Approximately 30km north of Florence is the Ferrari-owned track, **Mugello** (☎ 055 849 91 11; www.mugellocircuit.it; Via Senni 15, Scarperia), which hosts regular Formula 3000 car racing and the world-championship motorcycle competitions in early summer. Tickets for one day of championship motorcycle racing cost from €60 to €175. The nearest train station is at Borgo San Lorenzo.

SUMMER FROLICS

The fun doesn't stop just because phalanxes of entertainment venues close during the summer (especially in July and August); it just moves outdoors.

Bring along your swimming gear to **Le Pavoniere**, the pool in the Parco delle Cascine (1, D2) park that from 8pm to 2am (especially on Thursday) turns into an open-air dip-and-sip session that attracts people from all over town.

In **Piazza di Santo Spirito** (4, A7) a bar is set up in the middle of the square every night for Notti d'Estate (Summer Nights) and frequent live-music acts keep punters coming. The (free) fun lasts from 8pm to 1am. A similar scene is played out at the other end of town in **Piazza Ghiberti** (7, C4), stage for the Sant'Ambrogio Summer Festival. Rime Rampanti is a mixed programme of music and theatre on **Piazza Giuseppe Poggi** by the Porta San Niccolò in Oltrarno (7, C6).

Sleeping

Florence is brimming with good places to stay, ranging from magnificently lavish *palazzi* to cosy *pensioni;* the problem is, there are even *more* overpriced and mediocre joints so you have to select your shelter carefully.

Book in advance for peak times (April to June, September to October, Christmas) or for *any* period if you have a particular place in mind. Demand drops during the hottest months of July and August, when Italians head to the hills and the beaches, and leave city sweltering to those who don't know better.

The city's one- to five-star rating for hotels relates only to their facilities only, and gives no indication of value, comfort or atmosphere.

Our price guide is for high-season rates, effective from Easter to mid-October and the Christmas–New Year period, although some places drop their prices in the hotter months, while others stick with the same rates year round. Whatever time of year, if business seems slow it's worth haggling for a better rate (and you may get a discount at midrange places if you pay with cash instead of card). Breakfast in cheaper accommodation is rarely worth a bleary eye so, if you have the option, save a few bob and pop into a bar for a coffee and *brioche* (pastry) as the Florentines do.

Waiting to make a Grand (p70) entrance

DELUXE

Grand Hotel (3, B6)
The public areas blend into an immense, opulent hall with a stained-glass ceiling, marble floors and, frankly, too much extravagant frippery. The richly coloured rooms are more tasteful, while the more expensive ones are adorned with frescoes and decked out in early-Florentine style. The equally breath-taking **Excelsior** (3, B6; ☎ 055 2 71 51; ⌨ www.starwood.com ⊠ Piazza d'Ognissanti 3 🚌 A & B 🚹 🗶 Il Cestello 🚶) across the square is run by the same multinational. ☎ 055 2 71 61 ⌨ www.starwood.com ⊠ Piazza d'Ognissanti 1 🚌 A & B 🅿 €42-55 🗶 InCanto 🚶

Grand Hotel Minerva (4, A2)
Barely a stumble with your wheel-propelled luggage from the train station, this magnificent spot offers some unbeatable trump cards.

LONG-TERM RENTAL
If you are staying a week or longer, consider renting an apartment. You can be looking at €500 per week or more. Longer term rents are proportionately cheaper – say €800 per month for a central studio. **In Florence** (www.inflorence.co.uk) has small flats starting at €1000 per month. For upper-end options, try **Florence & Abroad** (3, D3; ☎ 055 48 70 04; www.florenceandabroad.com; Via San Zanobi 58).

Forget the noise outside and slumber in the internal garden. Go for a dip amid the views at the hotel pool. ☎ 055 2 72 30 ⌨ www.grandhotelminerva.com ⊠ Piazza di Santa Maria Novella 16 🚌 1, 7, 10, 11, 14, 17, 22, 23, 36, 37 & A 🗶 I Chiostri 🚶

Helvetia & Bristol (4, C4)
If quality and refinement are top on your list, you won't pass this *belle-époque* gem, where each room is distinctly decorated with exquisite fabrics and charming antiques, while suites have sumptuous marble bathrooms and terraces.

☎ 055 2 66 51 ⌨ www.royaldemeure.com ⊠ Via dei Pescioni 2 🚌 6 & A 🅿 €30-35 🗶 Hostaria Bibendum

Hotel Lungarno (4, C7)
This luxury design hotel has one of the best locations in Florence, overlooking the Ponte Vecchio, and many rooms have tiny balconies jutting out over the river. The lobby bar has a wall of windows that makes full use of the view, and is a lovely spot for a drink or afternoon tea. ☎ 055 2 72 61 ⌨ www.lungarnohotels.com ⊠ Borgo San Jacopo 14 🚌 D 🅿 €32 🚹 🗶 Borgo San Jacopo 🚶

Hotel Savoy (4, D4)
Built in 1893 but completely transformed in 2000, the super-slick Savoy is one of the most central luxury lodgings in town – appealing to business travellers *and* tourists. It has stylishly minimalist modern interiors with pale hues offset by bold dashes of colour. Rooms are spacious – some even have walk-in closets or small balconies. ☎ 055 2 73 51 ⌨ www.roccofortehotels.com ⊠ Piazza della Repubblica 7 🚌 A 🅿 🚹 🗶 L'Incontro 🚶

The stylish Hotel Savoy

Palazzo Magnani Feroni
(3, B6)
Seven sumptuously decorated suites, each with a marble bathroom, spread across the beautifully restored 16th-century *palazzo* of the aristocratic Feroni family. It has all the facilities of a five-star, plus magnificent views from its roof terrace, although the atmosphere is more like that of a private apartment.
☎ 055 239 95 44 ☐ www .florencepalace.it ✉ Borgo San Frediano 5 🚌 6 & D ✕ Momoyama

TOP END

Gallery Hotel Art (4, C6)
If you dig design and comfort in equal measures, then this stop (run by the same folk as Hotel Lungarno) on the 'alley of gold', next to Ponte Vecchio, is the perfect choice. It has Asian minimalist décor, a lobby that serves as a gallery space, linen hand towels, and a library/lounge perfect for playing the recalcitrant rock star.
☎ 055 2 72 63 ☐ www .lungarnohotels.com ✉ Vicolo dell'Oro 5 🚌 B 🅿 €32 ♿ ✕ Fusion Bar 🚼

Grand Hotel Baglioni
(4, B2)
Timber-beam ceilings, dark wood furnishings and parquet floors and lend the rooms here a particular warmth in spite of the place's size (193 rooms),

Now that's a room with a view – Grand Hotel Baglioni

while the public areas in *pietra serena* (grey 'tranquil stone') have a softly grander tone. The rooftop restaurant and garden offer stirring views.
☎ 055 2 35 80 ☐ www .hotel-florencia.hotelbag lioni.it ✉ Piazza dell'Unità Italiana 6 🚌 1, 7, 10, 11, 14, 17, 22, 23, 36, 37 & A 🅿 €35-40 ♿ ✕ Terrazza Brunelleschi 🚼

Hotel Brunelleschi (4, E4)
Sleep where the Romans once bathed. Well almost. In the basement of the medieval tower around which this hotel has been constructed are the remains of the Roman baths. Your own bath will be somewhat more up to date! Try for a room on the upper floors. In the tower you can hang in the bar or use the wi-fi business facilities.
☎ 055 2 73 70 ☐ www .hotelbrunelleschi.it ✉ Piazza Santa Elisabetta 3 🚌 A 🅿 €30 ✕ Gustavino 🚼

Hotel Monna Lisa (7, B3)
This Renaissance palazzo seems to bristle, jealously guarding its Mediterranean garden and centuries-old rooms. Owned by relatives of the 19th-century sculptor Giovanni Dupré, some of whose works are scattered about the place, the hotel is a gentle haven. Rooms are smallish but homely and tastefully decorated.
☎ 055 247 97 51 ☐ www .monnalisa.it ✉ Borgo Pinti 27 🚌 14 & 23 🅿 €15 ♿ ✕ Caffellatte

JK Place (4, B3)
One of the cutest of Florence's small but growing bevy of designer digs, JK Place is a modest-looking affair from the outside with 20 quite individual rooms. You might sleep in four-poster majesty or enjoy a marble fireplace. Designer touches are a mix of styles and rooms are painted in warm, soothing colours.
☎ 055 2664 51 81 ☐ www.jkplace.com ✉ Piazza di Santa Maria Novella 7 🚌 1, 7, 10, 11, 14, 17, 22, 23, 36, 37 & A ✕ The Lounge

CHILD'S PLAY
Most hotels – apart from the budget places – cater for kids and have ready access to babysitting services and cots. Look for the child-friendly icon 🚼.

Hotel Monna Lisa (p71)

MIDRANGE

Albergo La Scaletta
(4, C7)
You'd never guess it from the inside but this homely hotel is situated on one of Florence's busiest tourist thoroughfares. Although only a few rooms have private facilities, those at the back look onto the Giardino di Boboli, and a wonderful sun-kissed roof terrace provides the full 360 degrees.
☎ 055 28 30 28 ▢ www .lascaletta.com ✉ Via de' Guicciardini 13 🚌 D 🍴 Le Volpi e l'Uva ♿

Aprile (4, A2)
Housed in a former Medici *palazzo* – that's Cosimo above the entrance – this small and sometimes charming hotel feels like a pair of comfortable old slippers. Rooms vary from the large and frescoed to the cramped and gloomy. If you and your zzzzs are easily parted, get a back room overlooking the shaded courtyard.
☎ 055 21 62 37 ▢ www .hotelaprile.it ✉ Via della Scala 6 🚌 11, 36, 37

& A 🍴 Osteria dei Cento Poveri ♿

Hotel Bellettini (4, C2)
One of the best midrange joints in town, this hospitable hotel occupies a *palazzo* that has been providing shelter to travellers for almost four centuries. Room No 45 has splendid views of the Cappelle Medicee and the Duomo's dome.
☎ 055 21 35 61 ▢ www .hotelbellettini.com ✉ Via de' Conti 7 🚌 1, 6, 7, 10, 11 & 17 🍴 Ristorante Self-Service Leonardo ♿

Hotel Casci (4, E1)
The 25 rooms at this central hotel, which is housed in a 15th-century *palazzo*, are plain but cosy and quiet. Frescoes adorn the public rooms and a sociable atmosphere pervades the place, but the best reason to stay here is the friendly family who run it.
☎ 055 21 16 86 ▢ www .hotelcasci.com ✉ Via Cavour 13 🚌 1, 6, 7, 10, 11 & 17 🅿 €23-27 ♿
🍴 Trattoria Mario ♿

Hotel Il Guelfo Bianco
(3, D4)
Friendly welcoming staff, pretty décor and a central location make for a winning combo in this hotel, made up from two adjacent 15th-century *palazzi*. It's on a busy, central street

but noise isn't a problem because the windows are triple-paned and some of the back rooms overlook quiet courtyards.
☎ 055 28 83 30 ▢ www .ilguelfobianco.it ✉ Via Cavour 57/r 🚌 1, 6, 7, 10, 11 & 17 🅿 €24-30 ♿
🍴 Trattoria Mario ♿

Hotel Loggiato dei Serviti (7, A1)
Architectural buffs will probably already be booked into the front rooms of this delightful hotel, a 16th-century monastery facing Brunelleschi's Spedale degli Innocenti across one of Florence's most enchanting piazzas. The simple décor of the rooms enhances the fine 16th-century frescoes and painted plasterwork.
☎ 055 28 95 92 ✉ Piazza Santissima Annunziata 3 🚌 6, 31, 32 & C 🍴 Caffel-latte ♿

Hotel Tornabuoni Beacci
(4, C5)
You'll get faded glamour and a bright-eyed welcome at this small, Edwardian hotel on Florence's designer strip. Occupying the top three floors of a 15th-century *palazzo,* it has comfortable period-furnished rooms, modern bathrooms, a delightful roof terrace and a honeymoon suite decorated with 17th-century frescoes.

BETWEEN THE SHEETS
Couples should be aware that a *camera doppia* (double room) is generally taken to mean twin singles rather than a double bed. Stress that you want a *camera matrimoniale* (matrimonial room) and enjoy your lie-in.

When is a hotel a film set? When it's the Pensione Bandini.

☎ 055 21 26 45 ☐ www
.bthotel.it ✉ Via de'
Tornabuoni 3 🚌 6, 11, 36,
37 & A ♿ ✗ Ristorante
Tornabuoni Beacci ♿

Pensione Bandini (4, A8)
This rickety old gem is
flanked by a loggia overlooking Piazza Santo Spirito, one
of the liveliest and most local
squares in Florence. Many
of the rooms are large and
atmospheric – although
some of the beds haven't
aged so well – and there are
cosy guest lounges, which
you may recognise from the
film *Tea with Mussolini*.
☎ 055 21 53 08 🚌 Piazza
Santo Spirito 9 🚌 D
✗ Osteria Santo Spirito

Relais Uffizi (4, D6)
Overlooking Piazza della
Signoria, the de facto
centre of tourist Florence, this
relaxed hotel has a mixed
bag of rooms and is reached
via an ancient arch and lane
off Chiasso de' Baroncelli (a
useful escape route when you
need to flee the tour groups).
☎ 055 267 62 39 ☐ www
.relaisuffizi.it ✉ Chiasso del
Buco 16 🚌 B ♿ ✗ Vini e
Vecchi Sapori

BUDGET

Hotel Cestelli (4, C5)
Just around the corner from
the Arno, you couldn't be
closer to the heart of Florence in this charming, eight-
room family-run haven.
Singles are claustrophobic
but doubles are generous,
especially No 5, with its own
divan and window onto the
narrow street below.
☎ 055 21 42 13 ☐ www
.hotelcestelli.it ✉ Borgo SS
Apostoli 25 🚌 B ✗ Trat-
toria Coco Lezzone

Hotel San Giovanni
(4, D3)
It's a gloomy old walk up but
what a surprise on arrival
(who said the journey is more
important?). This Italian–

Australian–run digs is a gem.
The hotel was once part of
the bishop's private residence
(see the traces of fresco in
several rooms). Eight of the
nine rooms have views of the
Duomo and Battistero.
☎ 055 28 83 85 ☐ www
.hotelsangiovanni.com ✉ Via
de' Cerretani 2 🚌 1, 6, 7, 10,
11, 14, 17, 23 & A ✗ Ris-
torance Self-Service Leonardo

Hotel Scoti (4, C5)
If you'd rather spend your
lolly on boutiques than a
bed (or private bathroom),
bunk up in this atmospheric
pensione on Florence's most
prestigious shopping strip.
☎ 055 29 21 28
✉ hotelscoti@hotmail.com
✉ Via de' Tornabuoni 7
🚌 6, 11, 22, 36, 37 & A
✗ Trattoria Coco Lezzone

Residenze Johlea I & II
(3, E3)
With a total of 13 rooms
between them, these twin
pensioni offer impeccable,
individually decorated rooms
with mini-fridges. Johlea I,
which is at No 80 and acts
as reception for both, has a
gorgeous roof terrace.
☎ 055 463 32 92 ☐ www
.johlea.it ✉ Via San Gallo 76
& 80 🚌 1, 6, 7, 10, 11 & 17
♿ ✗ Il Vegetariano

THE TUSCAN HIGH-LIFE
If you want a taste of the Tuscan countryside while
staying close to downtown Florence, there are a few
places dotted on the hills surrounding the city. One of
the best is **Villa Poggio San Felice** (☎ 055 22 00 16;
http://poggiosanfelice.hotel-firenze.net; Via San Matteo in Arcetri 24), a tranquil, 15th-century villa nestled
in the hills of Pian dei Giullari behind Porta Romana,
about 5km south of the city centre. Twice-daily shuttles
operate into town.

HISTORY
Florentia
After crushing the Etruscan city of Fiesole, Julius Caesar established a garrison town in 59 BC for army veterans on the Arno, naming it Florentia (the Flourishing One). It prospered on maritime trade along the Arno until the Roman Empire collapsed in the 5th century.

Tuscany Takes Shape
In 774 Charlemagne, king of the Franks, began a campaign to boot out the squatting Lombards. By 800 he had been crowned head of the Holy Roman Empire, which took in the duchy of Tuscia – encompassing Tuscany, Umbria and much of Lazio. Under the 12th-century administration of Countess Matilda Canossa, the duchy gained virtual independence, but it descended into a free-for-all after her death, with rival cities jostling for dominance.

Guelphs & Ghibellines
Inter-family rivalries crystallised in the 13th century when Tuscany divided into the pro-imperial Ghibellines and the pro-papal Guelphs, broadly defined as the old nobility and merchant classes respectively. All hell broke loose in Florence following the murder in 1216 of the prominent Guelph Buondelmonte dei Buondelmonti over a broken engagement. The Guelphs eventually won and banished the Ghibellines from power. They warred with rival Ghibelline cities and adopted the red lily on a white background as the city's emblem (which survives today).

Despite the internal upheavals and battles with its neighbours, Florence prospered enormously through banking and textiles. By the beginning of the 14th century, it was one of the largest and wealthiest cities in Europe, with 100,000 inhabitants.

Plague, Upheaval & the Medici
Floods in 1333 and plague in 1348 wiped out half the city's population, and rising taxes prompted the short-lived 1378 Ciompi Revolt (*ciompi* referring to textile labourers). Warring with neighbouring cities continued too and by 1430 Florence controlled most of Tuscany.

Meanwhile, Giovanni di Bicci de' Medici steered his bank to become the largest operating in Europe. From 1434 his heir, Cosimo, became the de facto ruler of Florence and promoted intellectualism and famously, the arts. The artistic fervour gathered steam under Cosimo's grandson Lorenzo il Magnifico (r 1469–92). However, it seems he wasn't so magnificent with the books and, by the time Lorenzo died, the Medici were broke and the city of Florence was almost bankrupt.

NOT COLUMBUS' FAVOURITE PERSON
The Americas are named after Amerigo Vespucci, a Florentine navigator based in Seville, who first worked out that the land discovered by Genoa-born Christopher Columbus was a new continent and not India, as Columbus had obstinately believed.

From Hell to Unity

Florence briefly fell under the spell of Girolamo Savonarola (1452–98), a Dominican monk sent by God – so he reckoned – to cleanse the city of its extravagant, evil ways. At his direction, Florentines torched their books and finery on 'bonfires of the vanities'. When they later came to their senses, they torched him.

> ### CHEERS ANNA MARIA
> The last significant act of the Medici came in 1743 when the last of their number, Anna Maria Luisa (the daughter of Cosimo III), bequeathed all the Medici property and art to the rulers of Tuscany, on condition that it never leave Florence.

Niccolò Machiavelli (1469–1527) – a name synonymous with the dark side of politics – served in the Republican government that followed, but he and the Republic went by the wayside when the Medici returned.

A second-rate version of the Medici returned to power in 1512 and governed what degenerated into an insignificant provincial town. They fizzled out by 1737 and the Austrian House of Lorraine took over and knocked the place back into shape.

Florence slumbered along peacefully, showing off its treasure to the first waves of Grand Tourists. In 1860, Tuscany was incorporated into the Kingdom of Italy, of which Florence briefly became capital.

Modern Florence

The relative hardships of WWI helped bring Benito Mussolini (1883–1945) to prominence, and Florence became a violent Fascist stronghold between the wars. The city was badly damaged by the retreating German forces in WWII and the Ponte Vecchio was the only bridge spared.

Floods struck in 1966 and caused incalculable damage to Florence's buildings and artworks – although the city became a world centre for art restoration as a result. In 1993 a Mafia bomb caused substantial damage to the Uffizi Gallery, but it was patched up in record time so Florence could quickly get back to the business of making a buck out of its extraordinary past.

A quiet place to sketch on the reconstructed Ponte di Santa Trinitá

Not a parking inspector in sight

ENVIRONMENT

The biggest concern in tightly packed, scooter-crazy Florence is air pollution, both for the city's architectural heritage and its visitors. Traffic in the centre has been reduced, and gas and electric buses are helping but, even on a good day, Florence can choke. There's precious little green space downtown, especially on the northern bank, while the incessant rattling of two-stroke engines is enough to jangle the nerves of Buddha.

If it starts to get you down, head to the hills above San Niccolò in the Oltrarno, where you can wander into what feels like typical Tuscan countryside. As you walk along the river, know that the 2ft beast on the banks is the local *norvegicus* rat that lives in the city's sewerage pipes!

GOVERNMENT & POLITICS

Florence is the capital of Tuscany, one of the 20 regions of Italy. The state-funded regional parliament *(consiglio regionale)* legislates on a limited range of issues, such as tourism and the hospitality industry.

Tuscany is divided into 10 provinces, each named after its respective capital and further subdivided into local administrative districts *(comuni)*. The *comune* of Florence takes in a relatively small area, identified by road signs leading out of the city showing a red line through 'Firenze'. It comprises five local councils *(quartieri)*, and since July 1999 has been headed by mayor *(sindaco)* Leonardo Domenici, who fronts a centre-left coalition led by the former communists, the Democratici di Sinistra (DS).

As elsewhere in Italy, it pays to be connected to the right people; as the left has ruled virtually continuously since WWII, anyone who wants to get anywhere tends to have party affiliations. Although the DS have long called themselves communists, they bear (and bore) little similarity to those of the former East Bloc. Left-wing in name, Florentines are by nature rather more conservative and entrepreneurial.

ECONOMY

In 1189 Florence gave the world the silver *fiorino* (florin), a currency bearing the lily of Florence and the bust of its patron saint, St John the Baptist. By the time it started to mint the gold version in 1253, the city had an international reputation

DID YOU KNOW?
The *comune* of Florence totals 368,000 inhabitants (among them 32,000 foreigners) and the city's per capita GDP is around €18,000, with unemployment among the country's lowest at 4.2%.

for banking expertise and fiscal nous after inventing double-entry book-keeping and a forerunner to the cheque.

The city has historically rejected industrialisation, preferring instead to rely on artisan products, textiles, financial services and, of course, tourism, which plays an enormous role in the local economy. Some three million people visit each year, pouring up to US$2 billion into the local economy.

SOCIETY & CULTURE

Other Italians, not exactly slobs themselves, like to rib Florentines about their preoccupation with *bella figura* (looking good), a term encompassing much more than sartorial splendour. In many regards, they're a conservative bunch and keep largely to themselves. Under constant siege from tourists, most are courteous and friendly, but some tolerate us the way a carpenter would splinters.

People don't expect you to speak Italian but will warm to you more quickly if you good-humouredly fumble your way through a few phrases.

Although many residents are migrants from elsewhere in Italy, there is virtually nothing in the way of cuisine from other regions to sample. Other resident blow-ins include clusters of Roma families, largely treated like second-class citizens, as well as communities from Africa, Albania, Romania and the Philippines.

About 85% of Florentines – and Italians – are Catholic, with the remainder made up of Muslims, Protestants and a sizable chunk of Buddhists. Hope in the local Muslim community that the city might finally have a proper mosque was fuelled by apparent consensus in the municipality on the idea. Given how long it seems to take the city to execute urban projects, no-one is holding their breath.

So much to do, so little time

Painting on walls is a fine art in Florence

Etiquette

Florentines are used to *stranieri* (foreigners) and it's difficult to make a faux pas. The most common way tourists offend local sensibilities – apart from their fashion sense – is by baring too much flesh. You won't be allowed in to some churches if you're inadequately attired. Shorts (that aren't too skimpy) are usually okay, but cover your shoulders and don a little sensitivity.

Smoking is banned in all public, enclosed spaces, including restaurants and bars.

ARTS

Florence is known above all for the flowering of the arts that took place in the 15th and 16th centuries, the Renaissance (literally 'rebirth'). Its innovations in construction also helped revolutionise architecture around Europe. Literature too flourished and Italian overtook Latin as a literary tool.

Architecture

The seeds of the Florentine Renaissance were sown with the works of the Romanesque and Gothic periods. The best remaining examples of Romanesque architecture are the Battistero and the mystical Chiesa di San Miniato al Monte. The grand basilicas of Santa Croce and Santa Maria Novella are the city's two great Gothic churches. Santa Croce was the work of the Siena-born Arnolfo di Cambio (1245–1302), who also designed the Duomo and the fortresslike Palazzo Vecchio, the centre of municipal power then and now.

CULTURAL CAPITAL

According to Unesco, some 60% of the world's most important works of art are located in Italy, and approximately half of these are in Florence.

Filippo Brunelleschi (1377–1446) launched Renaissance architecture when he erected the majestic dome for the Duomo, using hitherto untried building methods to create a unique addition to the urban skyline. He also designed the city's great Renaissance churches, the **Santo Spirito** (p29) and **San Lorenzo** (p16) basilicas.

Michelangelo Buonarroti (1475–1564) also dabbled in architecture and his contributions to Florence are crowned by the **Sagrestia Nuova** in the Basilica di San Lorenzo and the **Biblioteca Medicea Laurenziana** in the same church complex. Giorgio Vasari (1511–74) created the **Uffizi** (p8).

The most exciting architecture in recent times has been in train stations. **Stazione di Santa Maria Novella**, an innovative number built in the Fascist heyday was thought a daring project at the time. It will be upstaged by Sir Norman Foster's project for a new high-speed train station.

Painting & Sculpture

Giotto (1266–1337) was ahead of his time as a Gothic-era painter who explored more natural, expressive forms through his grasp of perspective. He also designed the Campanile (bell tower) to accompany the Duomo. More firmly rooted in the Gothic tradition was Andrea Pisano (1290–1348), creator of the bronze doors on the south side of the Baptistery.

Lorenzo Ghiberti (1378–1455) spent 27 years on producing the set of 10 extraordinary Renaissance panels for the Baptistery that Michelangelo later dubbed the Gates of Paradise.

Donatello (c 1386–1466) probably shares with Michelangelo the title for greatest Renaissance sculptor in the city. His exquisite bronze *David,* in the Museo Nazionale del Bargello bears up well to Michelangelo's like-named marble masterpiece in the Galleria dell'Accademia.

In painting, Masaccio (1401–28) was one of the first to really cut loose from Gothic ties. His frescoes in the Cappella Brancacci introduced the profound, raw emotion that laid the groundwork for a whole generation of artistic genius.

The roll call seems as limitless as the Russian steppes: Dominican friar Fra Angelico (1395–1455) brought the lessons of perspective to religious painting, particularly in what is now the Museo di San Marco; Domenico Ghirlandaio (1449–94) produced the uncharacteristically savage *Strage degli Innocenti* (Massacre of the Innocents) in the Basilica di Santa Maria Novella; Sandro Botticelli (1445–1510) painted elegant and dreamy masterpieces such as the *Nascita di Venere* (Birth of Venus), now in the Uffizi. Leonardo da

An original bronze panel of the Battistero (p11), at Museo dell'Opera del Duomo (p13)

Pavement chalk art – is this the work of a modern-day master?

Vinci (1452–1519) tried his hand at everything and left behind some masterpieces in the Uffizi; Filippo Lippi (c 1406–69) and his son Filippino (1457–1504) left works behind across the city; and sculptor Luca della Robbia (1400–82) turned his hand to calling-card glazed terracotta sculptures.

Michelangelo went above and beyond the Renaissance, launching mannerism and leaving behind marvels such as *Tondo Doni* in the Uffizi.

It did not stop there. In Michelangelo's formidable footsteps followed Andrea del Sarto (1486–1530), Jacopo Pontormo (1494–1556), Il Rosso Fiorentino ('the Florentine Redhead'; 1495–1540), Il Bronzino (1503–72). Key sculptors included Benvenuto Cellini (1500–71), Bartolommeo Ammannati (1511–92) and Flemish-born Giambologna (Jean de Boulogne; 1529–1608).

Florentine art went into decline thereafter, then was briefly galvanised by the 19th-century Macchiaioli movement, a sort of local branch of French impressionism.

Literature

As in the visual arts, Florence was the cradle of a literary revolution. It was here that three great writers, Petrarch (1304–74), Boccaccio (1313–75) and especially Dante Alighieri (1265–1321) raised Italian to the status of a rich literary vehicle, largely abandoning Latin in its favour. This revolution was primarily due to Dante's *La Divina Commedia* (The Divine Comedy), an extraordinary work of political and social commentary and literary genius.

Directory

ARRIVAL & DEPARTURE

Since Florence's own airport is limited, passengers have a further two choices, Pisa and Bologna, both linked to Florence by rail. Indeed, Florence is strategically located on the country's main north–south rail route between Milan and Rome. Bus services run regularly into the hinterland.

Air

Domestic and European flights serve Florence's Amerigo Vespucci airport, 5km west of the centre. Numbers are limited, though, and you may find it more convenient to opt for the main regional hub, Pisa's Galileo Galilei airport. A further option is Bologna's Guglielmo Marconi airport, now served by low-cost flights from the UK. Both cities are within about 1½ hours' train travel from Florence.

AMERIGO VESPUCCI AIRPORT, FLORENCE
Information
Flight ☎ 055 306 13 00
Airport 🖳 www.aeroporto.firenze.it

Airport Access

The Volainbus shuttle bus (€4, 25 minutes) runs every half-hour from 5.30am to 8pm and then hourly to 11pm between the airport and the SITA bus terminal (3, B5). A taxi to the city centre will cost around €15.

GALILEO GALILEI AIRPORT, PISA
Left Luggage
There are **left-luggage facilities** (per piece per day €6; 🕓 8am-8pm) at the tourist information desk in the arrivals hall.

Information
Flight ☎ 050 84 93 00
Airport 🖳 www.pisa-airport.com

Airport Access

Local bus 3 goes to both central Pisa and the Pisa Centrale train station (€0.80, 15 minutes). The **Terravision** (www.terra vision.it) direct bus to Florence's Stazione di Santa Maria Novella runs 12 times daily (€7.50/13.50 one way/return) and takes 70 to 80 minutes one way. Eight direct trains connect Pisa's airport with Florence (€5, around 80 minutes), from 6.41am to 10.10pm. Otherwise, head for Pisa Centrale station.

GUGLIELMO MARCONI AIRPORT, BOLOGNA
Information
Flight ☎ 051 647 96 15
Airport 🖳 www.bologna-airport.it

Airport Access

The **Aerobus** (☎ 051 29 02 90) runs mostly every 15 minutes between Bologna's airport and central city train station (€4.50, 15 to 20 minutes). From there you can get a train to Florence. Plenty of trains run between Florence and Bologna (up to €13.17, one to 1½ hours).

Train

Florence's central station, **Stazione di Santa Maria Novella** (3, C4; ☎ 892021; www.trenitalia.it), is on the main line connecting Milan and Rome. There is a wide variety of services: the slower *locali*, *regionali* and *interregionali* trains are useful for exploring Tuscany, while the InterCity (IC) and Eurostar Italia trains will zip you to and from other major Italian cities. It's best (and in some cases obligatory) to book ahead for long-distance trips.

You can buy tickets, with either cash or credit card, from the automatic machines at stations, a quicker option than the ticket windows. Remember to validate your ticket using the yellow machine at the head of the platform or face an on-the-spot fine.

Left-luggage facilities are available. Look for the **deposito** (left luggage; per item for first five hours €3.80, then per hour €0.60 up until 12 hours, and thereafter per hour

€0.20 for maximum of five days; ⏱ 6am-midnight).

Bus
Bus is the best option for many Tuscan destinations, such as Siena. **Eurolines** (www.eurolines.com) runs the main international network, and services to Florence arrive at either the **SITA terminal** (3, B5; Piazza della Ztazione) or **Lazzi bus station** (3, F4; Piazza Adua), both near Stazione di Santa Maria Novella.

Travel Documents
PASSPORT
If you need a visa for Italy, your passport must be valid for several months after the date of entry.

VISA
EU citizens need only a passport or national ID card. Nationals of the USA, Canada, Australia, New Zealand, Israel and Japan don't need a visa if entering as tourists for up to three months. If you're not covered here – or you're a non-EU citizen entering Italy for any reason other than tourism – check with your Italian consulate, as you may need a specific visa.

Customs & Duty Free
Any goods over the duty-free limit must be declared. There are no limits, however, on the importation of euros. Non-EU citizens can import 200 cigarettes, 1L of spirits, 2L of wine and 60mL of perfume duty free.

GETTING AROUND
A stroll is usually all that's required to get around but when your feet need a holiday you can rely on local buses.

Travel Passes
Tickets for public transport cost €1 for one hour and €1.80 for three hours. A 24-hour ticket costs €4.50. A four-ticket set (*biglietto multiplo*) costs €3.90 (each ride valid for an hour). A new chip-card ticket, the

Carta Agile (€10/20 for 12/25 rides, each valid for an hour) is a further alternative for travellers.

Bus
ATAF (☎ 800 42 45 00) runs the local bus network. Several main bus stops surround Stazione di Santa Maria Novella (3, C4). Especially useful routes running from here include lines 7 (to Fiesole), 13 (to Piazzale Michelangelo) and 70 (a night bus to the Duomo and the Uffizi).

Four dinky and environmentally friendly buses whiz around the city centre (see Map 4). Lines A, B and C operate 8am to 8pm Monday to Saturday, while route D runs 7am to 9pm daily.

You can obtain route maps, schedules and passenger tickets from the ATAF Ticket & Information Office on Piazza della Stazione (3, C4).

Taxi
As a general rule, taxis (☎ 055 42 42, 055 47 98, 055 44 99, 055 43 90) can usually be found outside Stazione di Santa Maria Novella in Piazza della Stazione and at other ranks around the heart of Florence, particularly near Piazza Adua. The flagfall is €2.54, on top of which you pay €0.82 per kilometre within the city limits. Beyond the city, the rate is €1.47 per kilometre.

Car & Motorcycle
Driving and parking a car in central Florence is virtually impossible owing to the city's complex traffic restriction rules. Parking doesn't get much easier in the surrounding areas either. Your choices are between metered street parking or car parks. Among the cheapest options for a longer stay are those in Parterre (3, F2) and near Piazzale di Porta Romana (3, A9) in Oltrarno. Both cost €1.50 per hour or €15 for 24 hours.

Motorbikes and *motorini* (scooters) are the preferred mode of transport for (far too) many Florentines and can be taken into many areas closed to cars and parked quite easily.

HIRE
Along Borgo Ognissanti you'll find a cluster of local and international rental agencies, including **Happy Rent** (3, B5; ☎ 055 239 96 96; www.happyrent.com; Borgo Ognissanti 153/r). Starting prices for a small car are around €190 for three days or €355 for one week. The cheapest *motorino* will cost around €30 to €35 per day. If you want to drive in central Florence, consider hiring a tiny electric car or van from **Sologiallo** (☎ 055 28 39 14; www.sologiallo .it; Garage Europa, Borgo Ognissanti 96). These cars have a range of 100km, can be recharged for free at about 100 recharge points in Florence and cost from €18 an hour to €350 per week.

ROAD RULES
Italians drive on the right side of the road. Seat belts are compulsory, as are helmets for all motorbike and scooter riders. Use of dipped headlights is compulsory by day on highways. Speed limits are 50km/h in built-up areas, 90km/h on main roads and 130km/h on *autostrade*. Many petrol stations have self-service pumps that accept credit cards or notes. The blood-alcohol limit is 0.05%.

DRIVING LICENCE & PERMITS
Motoring EU citizens can use their normal driving licence. Everyone else is supposed to obtain an International Driving Permit.

Bicycle
Central Florence can be a picture from the saddle and is comparatively car-free. Beyond it can be a little more hairy. Exploring the hills of Chianti by bike is a popular activity, although you'll need strong calves and a hard butt to enjoy it fully!

Bike hire costs from €13 per day from **Florence by Bike** (3, D3; ☎ 055 48 89 92; Via San Zanobi 91/r and 120-122/r).

PRACTICALITIES
Business Hours
In general, shops open 9.30am to 1pm and 3.30pm to 7.30pm Monday to Saturday. They may remain closed on Monday morning or Saturday afternoon, or both afternoons.

Banks open 8.30am to 1.30pm and 3.30pm to 4.30pm Monday to Friday, but hours often vary.

Bars and cafés generally open 7.30am to 8pm, although some stay open after 8pm and turn into pub-style drinking places. Pubs and bars mostly shut by 1am, except on Friday and Saturday nights, when a few kick on until 2am or 3am.

For lunch most restaurants usually open from 12.30pm to 3pm; opening hours for dinner vary but generally people start sitting down to dine at around 8.30pm. It's difficult to find a place still serving after 10.30pm.

Climate & When to Go
Florence is a year-round destination though summers can sizzle and winters are cold and wet. July and August can be torrid when average highs nudge 31°C, there's not a breath of wind and many of the locals evacuate.

Winter, roughly from November to February, endures temperatures between 1°C and 10°C and rain that comes in weeks rather than showers.

Spring and autumn provide the most reliable and comfortable weather to be in Florence. With a bit of luck, you'll find the best all-round conditions in late April and early October. Easter, June and September are busy.

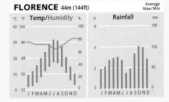

Disabled Travellers

Many older museums, restaurants, hotels and other venues will pose problems if you're wheelchair bound, while virtually all modern ones have adequate facilities. Most ATAF buses are equipped for wheelchair access; taxis take wheelchairs although you should mention your wheels when you book; and train carriages showing the wheelchair logo have facilities and adapted toilets.

INFORMATION & ORGANISATIONS

The Comune di Firenze (town council) publishes a booklet, *Guida alle Strutture e ai Servizi della Città*, which lists hundreds of places, including churches, museums, banks, hotels and restaurants, with an accessibility rating and description. The booklet comes with a map of central Florence outlining accessible footpaths and crossings for those in wheelchairs. It is sometimes available at the tourist offices. The council has similar information on its website under the tag NoBarriers. Another source of practical information is by Cornelia Danielson's *The Accessible Guide to Florence* (October 2004). She also runs **Barrier Free Travel Services** (☎ 055 233 61 28; www .bftservices.it; Via Benedetto da Foiano 19), which can help with organising a stay and tours in and around Florence.

Discounts

EU citizens under 18 and over 65 are entitled to free admission to all state and city museums, as well as discounted admission to private museums and sights. EU citizens between 18 and 25 get in half-price at state museums. Student-card holders – the International Student Identity Card (ISIC) is the most widely accepted – get discounts on a range of transport, accommodation and shops, but precious few sights.

Electricity

Voltage 220V
Frequency 50Hz
Cycle AC
Plugs standard continental two round pins

Embassies & Consulates

Should you get yourself in trouble – which isn't of your own making – the following embassies and consulates in Rome and Florence will be able to help.
Australia (☎ 06 85 27 21; Via Antonio Bosio 5, Rome)
Canada (☎ 06 44 59 81; Via G B de Rossi 27, Rome)
Ireland (☎ 06 697 91 21; Piazza Campitelli 3, Rome)
New Zealand (☎ 06 441 71 71; Via Zara 28, Rome)
UK (4, B5; ☎ 055 28 41 33; Lungarno Corsini 2, Florence)
USA (3, A5; ☎ 055 26 69 51; Lungarno Amerigo Vespucci 38, Florence)

Emergencies

Ambulance (ambulanza) ☎ 118
Fire brigade (vigili del fuoco) ☎ 115
Highway rescue (soccorso stradale) ☎ 116
Military police (carabinieri) ☎ 112
Police (polizia) ☎ 113

Fitness

Florentines love to watch sport but most are not keen on taking part. You'll get plenty of exercise walking between the sights, striding towards views, or cycling around the city. Other opportunities to get your endorphins pumping are largely limited to the gym, pool or a run around the Parco delle Cascine.

Palestra Ricciardi

(7, C2 ☎ 055 247 84 62 ⌨ www.pales trariccardi.com ✉ Borgo Pinti 75 € €10 ☺ 9am-10pm Mon-Fri, 9.30am-6pm Sat, closed Aug) A good central gym, this place has a full range of exercise machines, weights and classes

Piscina Nannini

(1, F3; ☎ 055 67 75 21 ✉ Lungarno Aldo Moro 6 € €6.50/4.50, book of 10 tickets €45 ☺ 10am-6pm Jun-Aug, entry by one-month subscription; limited hours Sep-May)

Just over 3km east of Ponte Vecchio along Lungarno Aldo Moro in Bellariva, this uncovered Olympic-size pool in summer provides the perfect tonic for torrid days.

Gay & Lesbian Travellers

Homosexuality is widely accepted although overt displays of affection might not go down well in rural towns and villages. In summer head for the gay clubs of Torre del Lago on the Versilia coast.

INFORMATION & ORGANISATIONS

ArciGay (www.arcigay.it), the national gay organisation, has general information on the gay and lesbian scene in Italy.

Azione Gay e Lesbica Finisterrae (3, A6; ☎ 055 22 02 50; www.azionegayelesbica .it, in Italian; Via Pisana 32/r) welcomes newcomers to town.

Ireos (3, B7; ☎ 055 21 69 07; www.ireos .org in Italian; Via de' Serragli 3/5; ☾ 5-8pm Mon-Fri) is a gay-lesbian association that organises cultural events and runs a medical counselling service.

Health

IMMUNISATIONS

No vaccinations are required for entry to Italy. The water is safe to drink.

INSURANCE & MEDICAL TREATMENT

Travel insurance is advisable to cover any medical treatment. EU citizens and those of countries such as Australia with reciprocal health-care agreements are entitled to the same basic free public health care as Italians on production of their European Health Insurance Cards (EHIC). All others will have to pay.

MEDICAL SERVICES

Ospedale di Careggi (1, D1; ☎ 055 427 71 11; Viale Morgagni 8)

Ospedale di Santa Maria Nuova (7; A2 ☎ 055 2 75 81; Piazza di Santa Maria Nuova 1)

Tourist Medical Service (3, D2; ☎ 055 47 54 11; Via Lorenzo il Magnifico 59)

PHARMACIES

The following pharmacies are open 24 hours:

All'Insegna del Moro (4, D3; ☎ 055 21 13 43; Piazza di San Giovanni 28)

Farmacia Comunale (3, C4; ☎ 055 21 67 61; Stazione di Santa Maria Novella)

Molteni (4, D5; ☎ 055 28 94 90; Via dei Calzaiuoli 7/r)

Holidays

1 January New Year's Day
6 January Epiphany
March/April Good Friday
March/April Easter Monday
25 April Liberation Day
1 May Labour Day
2 June Republic Day
15 August Feast of the Assumption
1 November All Saints' Day
8 December Feast of the Immaculate Conception
25 December Christmas Day
26 December St Stephen's/Boxing Day

Internet

If you're travelling with a laptop, make sure you know what you're doing and/or have a universal AC adaptor and a two-pin plug adaptor. Most local phone sockets now have the US RJ-11 type.

INTERNET SERVICE PROVIDERS

Major global ISPs have dial-in nodes in Italy; download a list of the numbers before you leave home. Otherwise you can open an account with a local ISP (if you have your own computer) or rely on cybercafés.

INTERNET CAFÉS

Many of Florence's cybercafés also offer cheap international calls, international package delivery and courier services. Expect to pay around €2.50 to €4.50 per hour at these and other places. Rates typically change according to length of use and time of day.

Internet Train (4, D5; ☎ 055 274 10 37; www.internettrain.it; Via Porta Rossa 38/r; ☾ 9.30am-midnight Mon-Sat,

10am-midnight Sun) There are 13 branches throughout town; some are marked on the maps.

Netgate (7, A3; ☎ 055 234 79 67; www.thenetgate.it; Via Sant'Egidio 14/r; ☻ 9am-11pm)

USEFUL WEBSITES
The Florence **APT office website** (www .firenzeturismo.it) offers the most comprehensive information for tourists in Florence.

The **Lonely Planet website** (www.lonely planet.com) provides a speedy link to many useful sites on Florence.

Lost Property
The lost-property office (*ufficio oggetti trovati*) is operated by the city council and the **local police** (*vigili urbani*; 1, D2; ☎ 055 328 39 42/43; Via Circondaria 19; ☻ 9am-noon Mon, Wed & Fri, 9am-noon & 2.30-4.30pm Tue & Thu) and is located northwest of the city centre.

Metric System
Italy uses the metric system rather than imperial and, like the rest of Continental Europe, Italians indicate decimals with commas and thousands with points. See the conversion table below.

TEMPERATURE
$°C = (°F - 32) ÷ 1.8$
$°F = (°C \times 1.8) + 32$

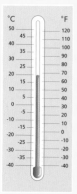

°C	°F
50	120
45	110
40	100
35	90
30	80
25	70
20	60
15	50
10	40
5	30
0	20
-5	10
-10	0
-15	-10
-20	-20
-25	-30
-30	-40
-35	
-40	

DISTANCE
1in = 2.54cm
1cm = 0.39in
1m = 3.3ft = 1.1yd
1ft = 0.3m
1km = 0.62 miles
1 mile = 1.6km

WEIGHT
1kg = 2.2lb
1lb = 0.45kg
1g = 0.04oz
1oz = 28g

VOLUME
1L = 0.26 US gallons
1 US gallon = 3.8L
1L = 0.22 imperial gallons
1 imperial gallon = 4.55L

Money
ATMS
Most banks in Florence have 24-hour cash-point machines (*bancomat*) that accept a wide variety of cards.

CHANGING MONEY
Banks and post offices offer better rates than the bureaux de change (*cambi*) that are dotted throughout tourist areas and whose commissions vary considerably. Also beware of 'no commission' signs, which usually indicate an inferior exchange rate.

CREDIT CARDS
Most places accept credit cards (although some smaller restaurants do not). Visa and MasterCard are the most widely accepted. For 24-hour card cancellations and assistance, call:

Amex ☎ 800 864 046
Diners Club ☎ 06 357 53 33 (Rome)
MasterCard ☎ 800 870 866
Visa ☎ 800 819 014

CURRENCY
Italy deals in euros. Coins come in denominations of 1, 2, 5, 10, 20 and 50 cents, and €1 and €2. The rather more useful notes are in denominations of €5, €10, €20, €50, €100, €200 and €500.

TRAVELLERS CHEQUES
Plastic is more practical than travellers cheques and some readers have reported difficulty getting them changed in some banks in Italy. If you still wish to use them (they are much safer than cash), Travelex, Amex and Visa are widely accepted. Take your passport when going to change them.

Newspapers & Magazines
You can get a wide range of international newspapers at newsstands all over Florence. There are no 'national' papers as such, but among the Italy's most important ones

are Milan's right-of-centre *Il Corriere della Sera* and Rome's left-of-centre *La Repubblica* (which has a good Florence insert). *La Nazione* is the main, conservative local option. For local news in English, track down *The Florentine,* a handy weekly distributed in English-language bookshops and other outlets.

The monthly *Firenze Spettacolo* has an English section and is good for listings and news of events and openings. The bimonthly *Florence – Concierge Information,* written in Italian and English and available free from tourist offices and hotels, has useful information for visitors.

Post
Italy's postal service, while still not the quickest in Europe, has improved considerably over the past years. Florence's **central post office** (4, C5; ☎ 803160; www.poste.it; Via Pellicceria; ☒ 8.15am-7pm Mon-Sat) is just off Piazza della Repubblica. *Francobolli* (stamps) are available from all post offices and *tabacchi* (tobacconists).

POSTAL RATES
Postcards and letters up to 20g sent *via aerea* (airmail) cost €0.45 within Europe, €0.65 to Africa, Asia, the Americas and €0.70 to Australia and New Zealand. Postcards cost the same. *Posta prioritaria* (priority post) is quicker and costs €0.62, €0.80 and €1 respectively.

Radio
The BBC World Service broadcasts on various frequencies (6.195MHz, 7320 MHz, 9.410MHz, 12.095MHz and 15.485MHz) depending on where you are and the time of day. Voice of America (VOA) can usually be heard on short wave at 1593MHz, 9685MHz, 11,835MHz, 15,255MHz and 17,555MHz.

There are three state-owned radio stations and they offer a combination of classical and light music with news broadcasts and discussion programmes: RAI-1

(87.8MHz FM), RAI-2 (90.5MHz FM) and RAI-3 (98.4MHz FM). For dance and indie music try Controradio (93.6MHz FM), or for a bit of world, jazz and soul try Nova Radio (101.5MHz FM).

Telephone
Calls in and from Italy are dearer from public payphones and hotels than from private phones. Public phones, liberally scattered throughout town, mostly accept phonecards (*carte/schede telefoniche;* €2.50 and €5). These are available at post offices, tobacconists and newsstands, and from vending machines in Telecom offices. Snap off the perforated corner before using it. A local call *(comunicazione urbana)* from a public phone costs €0.10 every minute and 12.5 seconds.

Phonecards offering reduced international rates can be bought at tobacconists, post offices, Internet cafés and some newsstands.

MOBILE PHONES
Italy uses the GSM cellular phone system, which is compatible with phones sold in just about every country except the USA and Japan. To use the network you must first set up a global roaming service with your service provider back home. It is possible to rent local phones at the Internet Train centres (see p85).

COUNTRY & CITY CODES
The area code for Florence is an integral part of the telephone number and must be dialled wherever you are.
Italy ☎ 39
Florence ☎ 055

USEFUL NUMBERS
International access code ☎ 00
Local directory inquiries ☎ 12
International directory inquiries ☎ 4176
International operator ☎ 170
Reverse-charge (collect) ☎ 170

Television

Italian TV is an excruciating mix of tacky game, talk and variety shows (with lots of tits and bums, crooning and vaudeville humour). The state-run RAI channels, particularly RAI-3, generally have the best programming. Canale 5 is the most popular private channel.

Time

Florence Standard Time is one hour ahead of GMT/UTC. Daylight-saving time is practised from the last Sunday in March to the last Sunday in October.

Tipping

Italians generally don't tip; some leave a few coins on the bar after a coffee but restaurant bills usually incorporate service charges. Where they don't, 10% is fair. Nobody tips taxi drivers but porters in the top hotels expect to have their palms crossed with silver and a couple of euro should do.

Tourist Information

APT (4, E1; ☎ 055 29 08 32; www .firenzeturismo.it; Via Cavour 1/r; 8.30am-6.30pm Mon-Sat, 8.30am-1.30pm Sun & holidays)

Comune di Firenze tourist office (4, A1; ☎ 055 21 22 45; Piazza della Stazione 4; 8.30am-7pm Mon-Sat & 8.30am-2pm Sun & holidays)

Comune di Firenze tourist office (7, A5; ☎ 055 234 04 44; Borgo Santa Croce 29/r; 9am-7pm Mon-Sat, 9am-2pm Sun & holidays Mar-Nov, 9am-5pm Mon-Sat, 9am-2pm Sun & holidays Dec-Feb)

Women Travellers

It isn't a dangerous city for women, but you might get un-wanted male attention, especially in bars and clubs. Avoid walking alone in deserted and dark streets, and look for a central hotel close to the action. The noticeboard at **Libreria delle Donne** (7, B3; ☎ 055 24 03 84; Via Fiesolana 2/b; 3.30-7.30pm Mon, 9.30am-1pm & 3.30-7.30pm Tue-Fri; bus 14, 23 & A) often has useful information.

LANGUAGE

As English and Italian share their Latin roots, you will recognise many Italian words. Florence was the birthplace of modern literary Italian in the 13th and 14th centuries, and the Florentine dialect was long considered the Italian standard (now something of a composite). Get Lonely Planet's *Italian Phrasebook* if you'd like to know more.

Basics

Hello.	Buongiorno. (pol)
	Ciao. (inf)
Goodbye.	Arrivederci. (pol)
	Ciao. (inf)
Yes.	Sì.
No.	No.
Please.	Per favore/
	Per piacere.
Thank you.	Grazie.
You're welcome.	Prego.
Excuse me.	Mi scusi.
Sorry. (forgive me)	Mi perdoni.
Do you speak English?	Parla inglese?
I don't understand.	Non capisco.
How much is it?	Quanto costa?

Getting Around

When does the ... leave/arrive?
A che ora parte/arriva ...?

bus	l'autobus
boat	la barca
train	il treno

I'd like a ... ticket.
Vorrei un biglietto di ...

one-way	solo andata
return	andata e ritorno

Where is ...?	Dov'è ...?
near/far	vicino/lontano
Go straight ahead.	Si va sempre diritto.
Turn left.	Giri a sinistra.
Turn right.	Giri a destra.

Accommodation

Do you have any rooms available?	Avete delle camere libere?
a hotel	un albergo
a room with bathroom	una camera con bagno
a ... room	una camera ...
single	singola
twin	doppia
double-bed	matrimoniale

Around Town

I'm looking for ...	
Cerco ...	
an ATM	un bancomat
the market	il mercato
a public toilet	un gabinetto
the tourist office	l'ufficio di turismo
What time does it open/close?	A che ora (si) apre/chiude?

Eating

breakfast	prima colazione
lunch	pranzo
dinner	cena
The bill, please.	Il conto, per favore.

Shopping

I'm just looking.	Sto solo guardando.
How much is it?	Quanto costa?
Do you accept ...?	
Accettate ...?	
credit cards	carte di credito
travellers cheques	assegni per viaggiatori

Time, Days & Numbers

What time is it?	Che ora è?
It's one/two o'clock.	È l'una/Sone le due.

today	oggi
tomorrow	domani
yesterday	ieri
morning	mattina
afternoon	pomeriggio
evening	sera
day	giorno
hour	ora
Monday	lunedì
Tuesday	martedì
Wednesday	mercoledì
Thursday	giovedì
Friday	venerdì
Saturday	sabato
Sunday	domenica
1	uno
2	due
3	tre
4	quattro
5	cinque
6	sei
7	sette
8	otto
9	nove
10	dieci
100	cento
1000	mille

Emergencies

Help!	Aiuto!
There's been an accident!	C'è stato un incidente!
I'm lost.	Mi sono perso. (m)
	Mi sono persa. (f)
Go away!	Lasciami in pace!
Call ...!	
Chiami ...! (pol)/Chiama ...! (inf)	
a doctor	un dottore/medico
the police	la polizia

Index

See also separate subindexes for Eating (p94), Entertainment (p94), Shopping (p94), Sights with map references (p95), and Sleeping (p95).

SIGHTS

SLEEPING

FEATURES

⊞ Procacci	*Eating*
⊡ Teatro Comunale	*Entertainment*
⊡ Capocaccia	*Drinking*
⊡ Sant'Ambrogio Caffè	*Café*
⊞ Palazzo Vecchio	*Highlights*
⊞ Pineider	*Shopping*
⊞ Casa di Dante	*Sights/Activities*
⊡ Hotel Monna Lisa	*Sleeping*

AREAS

	Beach, Desert
	Building
	Land
	Mall
	Other Area
	Park/Cemetery
	Sports
	Urban

HYDROGRAPHY

	River, Creek
	Intermittent River
	Canal
	Swamp
	Water

BOUNDARIES

	State, Provincial
	Regional, Suburb
	Ancient Wall

ROUTES

	Tollway
	Freeway
	Primary Road
	Secondary Road
	Tertiary Road
	Lane
	Under Construction
	One-Way Street
	Unsealed Road
	Mall/Steps
	Tunnel
	Walking Path
	Walking Trail/Track
	Pedestrian Overpass
	Walking Tour

TRANSPORT

	Airport, Airfield
	Bus Route
	Cycling, Bicycle Path
	Ferry
	General Transport
	Metro
	Monorail
	Rail
	Taxi Rank
	Tram

SYMBOLS

⑤	Bank, ATM
🛐	Buddhist
🏰	Castle, Fortress
✝	Christian
◤	Diving, Snorkeling
◒	Embassy, Consulate
✚	Hospital, Clinic
ⓘ	Information
@	Internet Access
☪	Islamic
✡	Jewish
🗼	Lighthouse
🔭	Lookout
▲	Mountain, Volcano
🏞	National Park
🅿	Parking Area
⛽	Petrol Station
•	Picnic Area
⊗	Point of Interest
⊗	Police Station
⊠	Post Office
⊗	Ruin
⊕	Telephone
🚻	Toilets
🐦	Zoo, Bird Sanctuary
🅝	Waterfall